9-11

A TRIBUTE

9-11

A TRIBUTE

Statements By:

Attorney General John Ashcroft, Secretary Of HHS Tommy Thompson, Secretary Of Transportation Norm Mineta,FEMA Director Joseph Allbaugh
President George W. Bush, Mayor Rudolph Giuliani, HRH Queen Elizabeth II, Governor George Pataki, Pope John Paul II
Prime Minister Tony Blair, President Jacques Chirac, Prime Minister Jean Chretien, King Abdullah II , President Vicente Fox, Chancellor Gerhard Schroeder
President Jiang Zemin, Prime Minister Atal Vajpayee, President Pervez Musharraf, President Vladimir Putin, Foreign Minister Jack Straw
Secretary Of State Colin Powell, Secretary Of Defense Donald Rumsfeld, Air Force Gen. Richard B. Myers, U.S. Deputy Defense Secretary Paul Wolfowitz
President Barack H. Obama

This revised edition published 2011 ISBN 978-1-84406-184-6
eBook edition ISBN 978-1-84406-185-3

All notations of errors or omissions should be addressed to
TAJ Books 27, Ferndown Gardens, Cobham, Surrey, UK, KT11 2BH, email: info@tajbooks.com.

First published in hardcover by Thunder Bay Press 2002 ISBN 1-57145-907-3

Pictures © Press Association

Library of Congress Cataloging-in-Publication Data available upon request.

Printed in China.
1 2 3 4 5 15 14 13 12 11

CONTENTS

The Attack 6

The Memorial 48

The President 80

The Prime Minister 110

The Mayor 122

World Leaders Unite 134

Attacking the Taliban 158

Epilogue 190

The Attack

Hijacked UA #175 Boeing 767 approaches the south tower of the World Trade Center; hijacked AA #11 Boeing 767 crashed into the north tower at 8:45 a.m., September 11, 2001, in New York.

PRESS BRIEFING BY ATTORNEY GENERAL JOHN ASHCROFT, SECRETARY OF HHS TOMMY THOMPSON, SECRETARY OF TRANSPORTATION NORM MINETA, AND FEMA DIRECTOR JOSEPH ALLBAUGH

SEPTEMBER 11, 2001

ATTORNEY GENERAL ASHCROFT: Today America has experienced one of the greatest tragedies ever witnessed on our soil. These heinous acts of violence are an assault on the security of our nation. They are an assault on the security and the freedom of every American citizen.

We will not tolerate such acts. We will expend every effort and devote all the necessary resources to bring the people responsible for these acts, these crimes, to justice.

Now is the time for us to come together as a nation to offer our support, our prayers for the victims and for their families, for the rescue workers, for law enforcement officials, for every one of us that has been changed forever by this horrible tragedy.

The following is a summary of the known facts surrounding today's incidents. American Airlines Flight 11 departed Boston for Los Angeles. Hijacked by suspects armed with knives, this plane crashed into the World Trade Center. United Airlines Flight 175 departed Boston for Los Angeles, was hijacked and crashed into the World Trade Center.

American Airlines Flight 77 departed Washington-Dulles for Los Angeles, was hijacked and crashed into the Pentagon. United Airlines Flight 93 departed Newark for San Francisco, was hijacked and crashed in Shanksville, Pennsylvania…

The determination of these terrorists will not deter the determination of the American people. We are survivors, and freedom is a survivor. A free American people will not be intimidated, nor will we be defeated. We will find the people responsible for these cowardly acts, and justice will be done.

SECRETARY THOMPSON: Every single American lost something today. And every one of us at this time expresses our deepest sympathy to the victims of today's tragedies, and their families.

It is now our mission to begin the healing from this tragedy. From the moment that we learned of these attacks, the Department of Health and Human Services has begun readying teams and resources to be sent to New York City and the Washington area to meet any needs of state and local officials…

A hijacked commercial plane crashes into the south tower of the World Trade Center at 9:05 a.m., September 11, in New York.

Americans all over are calling up and asking what they can do. The best thing they can do is respond to this great call by volunteering to give blood. We need Americans to continue to answer that call. No matter where you live, please, do your civic duty and assist us by donating blood. Our primary job is to make sure Americans, harmed by this tragedy, get the help that they need. We will remain in constant contact with the governors, the mayors, public health officials and other local officials to make sure that all their needs are being met.

It is a sad day, but America and all of its citizens certainly share tonight in the grief that has been caused. And as the President and everybody in his administration have said, we, the government, will continue to operate and continue to provide the services to all Americans.

SECRETARY MINETA: One of the most cherished freedoms is the freedom of movement, the ability to move freely and safely. But today, that freedom was attacked. But we will restore that freedom throughout the national transportation system as soon as possible. And we will restore the highest-possible degree of service.

These terrorist acts are designed to steal the confidence of Americans. We will restore that confidence. We have already taken some first steps as a precaution. I have ordered the FAA to ground all commercial air traffic until at least tomorrow afternoon. After the attack, some of our aircraft were diverted to Canada. And so we owe our Canadian neighbors a debt of gratitude for helping us as we redirected over 120 flights and their passengers to airports in Canada.

As of 6:00 p.m., Amtrak resumed its passenger rail service. Major railroads have taken steps to protect their assets as well. The United States Coast Guard is taking all necessary actions to control the movements of all vessels in navigable waters of the United States. Coast Guard helicopters have been assisting with medical and national security tasks.

We are currently looking at a wide variety of additional security measures to increase traveler security. Travelers will indeed see increased security measures at our airports, train stations, and other key sites. There will be higher levels of surveillance, more stringent searches. Airport curbside luggage check-in will no longer be allowed. There will be more security officers in random identification checks. Travelers may experience some inconveniences. But we ask for your

7

These photos taken by Space Imaging's IKONOS satellite, shows lower Manhattan before (June 30, 2000, above) and after (September 11, 2001, below) the terrorist attacks that destroyed the World Trade Center. The landmark Twin Towers can be seen at center-right.

patience. But we must do whatever it takes with safety as our highest priority. The Department of Transportation is working closely with the White House and appropriate federal agencies to mount a coordinated nationwide recovery effort. Each American must know that we will restore our national transportation system to a safe and efficient status as quickly as possible. Our system has been severely burdened by the stress of these horrendous attacks, but we will recover.

In a democracy, there is always a balance between freedom and security. Our transportation systems, reflecting the values of our society, have always operated in an open and accessible manner. And they will again. Please be assured that we are activating all of our resources on an emergency basis, and services will be restored as soon as possible.

DIRECTOR ALLBAUGH: Good evening. I activated this afternoon eight urban search and rescue task forces from all over the United States, and an incident support team, to arrive in New York. They are on their way as we speak. I've spoken with Governor Pataki, Governor Gilmore,

Mayor Giuliani; they are handling this about as well as anyone could handle it. These teams we've deployed are especially trained teams from all across the country, comprised of engineers and other technical individuals, with dogs that are trained to handle incidents such as this.

We at FEMA have also put a team on the ground, an advanced element team, who will be at the scene of the disaster probably as we speak. The Army Corps of Engineers are already on the ground, getting ready to handle debris removal.

This afternoon, as you know, the President did declare New York City a disaster. I have named Ted Monette the Federal Coordinating Officer. He will be my personal representative on the ground during the duration of this incident.

In Washington, as the Secretary said, we have three mortuary teams on site, three medical teams, four urban search and rescue teams. I believe this afternoon we shared with members of the media the names of those specific teams.

We will be deploying individuals as needed. I'll be in constant contact with those governors; additional search and rescue, if needed. We're identifying

additional needs that state and local governments are requiring.

As a result of the President's disaster declaration, tomorrow morning at 8:00 a.m., individuals who have been harmed may call our help line…We at FEMA will do all that we possibly can. After all, that is our job.

Our hearts are hurting this evening. Those individuals who have lost loved ones or do not know where their loved ones are, are in our prayers and are in our thoughts. Thank you all very much.

Lunchtime workers watch a giant screen in Martin Place, Sydney, Australia, September 12, 2001, showing graphic images of the Twin Towers of the World Trade Center in New York City after they were hit by two hijacked passenger jets.

"Just pray to God that we can save a few people."

—*Mayor Giuliani on arriving at the World Trade Center*

A view across the Hudson River showing the World Trade Center on fire. New York Mayor Rudolph Giuliani urged New Yorkers to evacuate lower Manhattan in an interview on NY1 television.

A U.S. flag flies in the foreground as one of the World Trade Center towers burns in the background.

A helicopter flies above the World Trade Center after the landmark Twin Towers were hit by two hijacked commercial aircraft.

Overview of New York after the north tower (WTC 1) has been hit by Flight 11

One of the towers of the World Trade Center begins to collapse.

The south tower of the World Trade Center collapses, sending dust and smoke into the streets.

I want to reassure the American people that the full resources of the federal government are working to assist local authorities to save lives and to help the victims of these attacks. Make no mistake: The United States will hunt down and punish those responsible for these cowardly acts.

I've been in regular contact with the Vice President, the Secretary of Defense, the national security team and my Cabinet. We have taken all appropriate security precautions to protect the American people. Our military at home and around the world is on high alert status, and we have taken the necessary security precautions to continue the functions of your government.

We have been in touch with the leaders of Congress and with world leaders to assure them that we will do whatever is necessary to protect America and Americans.

I ask the American people to join me in saying a thanks for all the folks who have been fighting hard to rescue our fellow citizens and to join me in saying a prayer for the victims and their families.

The resolve of our great nation is being tested. But make no mistake: We will show the world that we will pass this test. God bless.

—President George W. Bush,
September 11, 2001

"This is a vicious, unprovoked, horrible attack on innocent men, women, and children. It is one of the most heinous acts certainly in world history."

—Mayor Giuliani, September 11

The south tower of the World Trade Center collapses after being hit by a hijacked commercial aircraft.

New York police officers working hard to keep everyone calm and moving to safety.

A wall of dust and smoke races through the streets of lower Manhattan.

The north tower was hit by American Airlines Flight 11, impacting the 95th to 102nd floors.

Seventy-six passengers, nine flight attendants, two pilots, and five hijackers perished onboard.

The north tower collapsed one hour and forty minutes after impact.

The south tower was hit by United Airlines Flight 175, impacting the 86th to 92nd floors.

Fifty-one passengers, seven flight attendants, two pilots, and five hijackers perished onboard.

The south tower collapsed fifty-six minutes after impact.

People run as the top of one of the World Trade Center towers collapses.

View of lower Manhattan as the World Trade Center towers collapse.

Picture of the World Trade Center on 9/11 shortly after the second tower had collapsed.

A fire engine plows through the dust in the immediate aftermath of the destruction of the World Trade Center.

NYPD enter their temporary headquarters near the World Trade Center.

Firefighters enter the area around the now-destroyed World Trade Center.

Two emergency workers help a woman into a bus.

Rescue workers evacuate a man through rubble and debris.

A man covers his mouth as he walks
through debris.

An injured man waits for help as others
take refuge in a bank near the World
Trade Center towers.

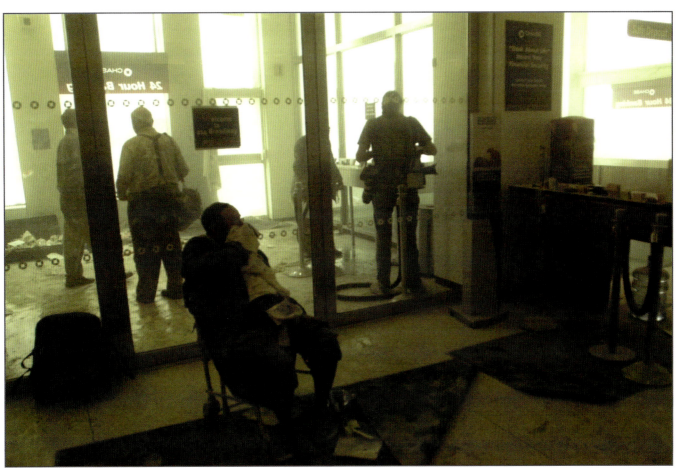

An exhausted police officer rests on a car covered in dust as people board a bus to be evacuated.

A fire fighter emerges from the smoke and debris of the World Trade Center.

Firefighters make their way through the rubble of the World Trade Center on September 11.

Queen Elizabeth II sent the following message to President George Bush after the tragic events of Tuesday, September 11:

"It is with growing disbelief and total shock that I am learning of the terrorist outrages in New York and Washington today. On behalf of the British people, Mr. President, may I express my heartfelt sympathy to the very many bereaved and injured and our admiration for those who are now trying to cope with these unfolding tragedies. Our thoughts and prayers are with you all."

View of the Pentagon from the Navy Annex minutes after a hijacked jetliner crashed into building at approximately 0930 on September 11, 2001.

Smoke billows from the Pentagon.

Firefighters and engineers examine the damaged side of the Pentagon on September 12.

The Pentagon in flames moments after a hijacked jetliner crashed into building at approximately 0930 on September 11, 2001.

View of the Pentagon from the Navy Annex minutes after a hijacked jetliner crashed into the building at approximately 0930 on September 11, 2001.

Department of Defense workers from the Navy Annex evacuate the building, minutes after a hijacked jetliner crashed into the Pentagon on September 11, 2001.

Aerial view of the Pentagon Building located in Washington, District of Columbia (DC), showing emergency crews responding to the destruction caused when a high-jacked commercial jetliner crashed into the southwest corner of the building, during the 9/11 terrorists attacks.

Shot of the exposed wreckage after the smoke cleared from a hijacked jetliner which crashed into the Pentagon at approximately 0930 on September 11, 2001.

*US President George W. Bush visits
the Pentagon on September 12, 2001.
Secretary of Defense Donald H. Rumsfeld
briefs him, in the aftermath of the
September 11th terror attack.*

*US President George W. Bush visits
the Pentagon to survey damage and
commend the joint rescue and recovery
efforts currently underway the following
the September 11, 2001, terrorist attack.*

President George W. Bush (center) and Secretary of Defense Donald Rumsfeld (center left) tour the impact area of the Pentagon late September 12. Bush said he was "overwhelmed" by the destruction.

This September 12 photo by Space Imaging's IKONOS satellite shows the Pentagon (center) in Arlington, one day after a passenger plane controlled by hijackers crashed into the building (top part of the Pentagon).

An overall aerial view, two days later, of the impact point on the Pentagon where the hijacked American Airlines Flight 77, a Boeing 757-200 entered, breaking up in the process.

The moon rises as rescue workers continue to fight fires and inspect the damage at the Pentagon, September 12.

"Jeremy Glick of Flight 93. His courage and self-sacrifice may have saved the White House."
—President Bush

Investigative personnel, looking for debris and evidence, including the plane's flight recorder, search the crash site of hijacked UA #93 Boeing 757, which crashed at 10:03 A.M. killing all 45 people on board, in Shanksville, Pennsylvania.

A Proclamation

As a mark of respect for those killed by the heinous acts of violence perpetrated by faceless cowards upon the people and the freedom of the United States on Tuesday, September 11, 2001, I hereby order, by the authority vested in me as President of the United States of America by the Constitution and the laws of the United States of America, that the flag of the United States shall be flown at half-staff at the White House and upon all public buildings and grounds, at all military posts and naval stations, and on all naval vessels of the Federal Government in the District of Columbia and throughout the United States and its Territories and possessions until sunset, Sunday, September 16, 2001. I also direct that the flag shall be flown at half-staff for the same length of time at all United States embassies, legations, consular offices, and other facilities abroad, including all military facilities and naval vessels and stations.

IN WITNESS WHEREOF, I have hereunto set my hand this eleventh day of September, in the year of our Lord two thousand one, and of the Independence of the United States of America the two hundred and twenty-sixth.

—*GEORGE W. BUSH*

Photographs of an airplane part found at the scene in Somerset County, Pennsylvania, where Flight 93 crashed.

Firemen and rescue personnel work at ground zero on September 14 in New York.

(Sep. 14, 2001) -- What is left of the south tower of the World Trade Center in New York City, stands like a tombstone among the debris and devastation caused by the Sep. 11, terrorist attack.

Photographs of an airplane parts found at the scene in Somerset County, Pennsylvania, where Flight 93 crashed.

People gather to give support to the rescue workers at their staging area on the pier at Clarkson St. and West St. on September 13. The workers are toiling away at the now collapsed World Trade Center.

"The number of casualties will be more than most of us can bear,"

a visibly distraught Mayor Rudolph Giuliani said.

"The best way to deal with this is not only to deal with our own grief,"

the mayor told reporters,

"but also show we're not cowered by it, that we're not afraid and go about our business."

Taken on September 14, this picture shows shattered window frames from the devastation that was once the World Trade Center in New York City.

A canine officer and his dog rest after search duty on September 18 at the site of last week's World Trade Center terrorist attack. Beliefs that the basement of the World Trade Center may contain some pockets of air, and possibly survivors, offer a faint glimmer of hope to weary workers as they begin their second week of rescue operations.

A firefighter standing amid the devastation that was once the World Trade Center in New York City. (opposite)

GOVERNOR GEORGE PATAKI'S REMARKS TO THE JOINT SESSION OF THE NEW YORK STATE LEGISLATURE

SEPTEMBER 13, 2001

Today, we join together as a State, and as a Nation, to pray for the victims who were lost on one of the darkest days in American history.

We pray for the children who will go to bed this evening without their mothers and fathers. We pray for the mothers and fathers who've lost the children they loved. We pray for the husbands and wives who will return to empty homes. We pray for the firefighters, police officers, and rescue workers who died while commiting extraordinary acts of heroism.

We pray, also, for this great nation of ours, a nation that is free, a nation that is strong, a nation that is united in grief. For we know that the freedom we so cherish as Americans—for which hundreds of thousands of Americans have sacrificed their lives—exposes us to the wicked, the murderous, the cowardly forces of hate.

December the 7th will always be known as a "Day of Infamy" so, too, September 11, from henceforth will be known as the day a dark cloud descended across America. But clouds always pass. The sun always breaks through. And we know as Americans that God's light will again shine across this land, and that our free and strong people will prevail.

The forces of evil that commited this atrocity have caused pain that will last for generations, pain that has claimed the lives of innocent men, women and children. But evil never prevails. Freedom, despite its vulnerabilities, will always prevail.

And I am confident that President Bush and a united American Congress will strike back—swiftly and strongly—against the forces of terror and the nations that harbor them. We will stand with the President in those actions.

New Yorkers have always stood strong, firm and together in times of crisis and human hardship. Already, we've seen the extraordinary heroism of our firefighters, police officers, rescue workers, and everyday citizens. We've seen the indomitable spirit of New Yorkers, pulling together to overcome the most horrendous, destructive, and murderous act of terrorism in history.

A series of aerial views showing the surrounding buildings which were heavily damaged by the debris and massive force of the falling twin towers.

Six World Trade Center, (US Customs
House) New York City, New York
View of southwest corner of the New York
Customs House

What was once a glittering symbol of the
financial center of the world now stands
blanketed in ash and soot.

Another Aerial shot showing the damage
to the towers and surrounding area.

The Memorial

I cannot begin this audience without expressing my profound sorrow at the terrorist attacks which yesterday brought death and destruction to America, causing thousands of victims and injuring countless people. To the President of the United States and to all American citizens I express my heartfelt sorrow. In the face of such unspeakable horror we cannot but be deeply disturbed. I add my voice to all the voices raised in these hours to express indignant condemnation, and I strongly reiterate that the ways of violence will never lead to genuine solutions to humanity's problems.

Yesterday was a dark day in the history of humanity, a terrible affront to human dignity. After receiving the news, I followed with intense concern the developing situation, with heartfelt prayers to the Lord. How is it possible to commit acts of such savage cruelty? The human heart has depths from which schemes of unheard-of ferocity sometimes emerge, capable of destroying in a moment the normal daily life of a people. But faith comes to our aid at these times when words seem to fail. Christ's word is the only one that can give a response to the questions which trouble our spirit. Even if the forces of darkness appear to prevail, those who believe in God know that evil and death do not have the final say. Christian hope is based on this truth; at this time our prayerful trust draws strength from it.

With deeply felt sympathy I address myself to the beloved people of the United States in this moment of distress and consternation, when the courage of so many men and women of good will is being sorely tested. In a special way I reach out to the families of the dead and the injured, and assure them of my spiritual closeness. I entrust to the mercy of the Most High the helpless victims of this tragedy, for whom I offered Mass this morning, invoking upon them eternal rest. May God give courage to the survivors; may he sustain the rescue-workers and the many volunteers who are presently making an enormous effort to

cope with such an immense emergency. I ask you, dear brothers and sisters, to join me in prayer for them. Let us beg the Lord that the spiral of hatred and violence will not prevail. May the Blessed Virgin, Mother of Mercy, fill the hearts of all with wise thoughts and peaceful intentions.

Today, my heartfelt sympathy is with the American people, subjected yesterday to inhuman terrorist attacks which have taken the lives of thousands of innocent human beings and caused unspeakable sorrow in the hearts of all men and women of good will. Yesterday was indeed a dark day in our history, an appalling offence against peace, a terrible assault against human dignity.

I invite you all to join me in commending the victims of this shocking tragedy to Almighty God's eternal love. Let us implore his comfort upon the injured, the families involved, all who are doing their utmost to rescue survivors and help those affected.

I ask God to grant the American people the strength and courage they need at this time of sorrow and trial.

At the end of the General Audience address, the Holy Father offered the following prayer of the faithful in Italian.

THE HOLY FATHER:

Brothers and Sisters, in great dismay, before the horror of destructive violence, but strong in the faith that has always guided our fathers, we turn to the God of Abraham, Isaac and Jacob, salvation of his people, and with the confidence of children, pray that He will come to our aid in these days of mourning and innocent suffering.

Holding his head in his hands Pope John Paul pauses in prayer during his weekly General Audience at the Vatican Wednesday 12th September 2001 when he renewed his condemnation of the devastating terrorist attacks on America, describing yesterday as a "dark day in the history of humanity".

"And I think people should be mournful and sorrowful, but they should also be very encouraged that we have tremendous courage in New York, we have tremendous courage in America, and the courage will be there in our generation as it was in prior generations."
Mayor Rudolph Giuliani.

In this photo obtained 18th September 2001 from the Federal Emergency Management Agency (FEMA), fire-fighters and Urban Search and Rescue workers battle smouldering fires as they search for survivors at the ruins of the World Trade Center in New York 13th September 2001. Rescue and recovery work continues at the site of the devastation in downtown Manhattan but hopes of finding anyone alive in the ruins of the World Trade Center have almost faded, New York Mayor Rudolph Giuliani said 18th September, one week after the terrorist attack that toppled the twin towers.

**PRESIDENT'S REMARKS AT NATIONAL DAY OF PRAYER AND REMEMBRANCE
THE NATIONAL CATHEDRAL
WASHINGTON, D.C.**

We are here in the middle hour of our grief. So many have suffered so great a loss, and today we express our nation's sorrow. We come before God to pray for the missing and the dead, and for those who love them.

On Tuesday, our country was attacked with deliberate and massive cruelty. We have seen the images of fire and ashes, and bent steel.

Now come the names, the list of casualties we are only beginning to read. They are the names of men and women who began their day at a desk or in an airport, busy with life. They are the names of people who faced death, and in their last moments called home to say, be brave, and I love you.

They are the names of passengers who defied their murderers, and prevented the murder of others on the ground. They are the names of men and women who wore the uniform of the United States, and died at their posts.

They are the names of rescuers, the ones whom death found running up the stairs and into the fires to help others. We will read all these names. We will linger over them, and learn their stories, and many Americans will weep.

To the children and parents and spouses and families and friends of the lost, we offer the deepest sympathy of the nation. And I assure you, you are not alone.

Just three days removed from these events, Americans do not yet have the distance of history. But our responsibility to history is already clear: to answer these attacks and rid the world of evil.

War has been waged against us by stealth and deceit and murder. This nation is peaceful, but fierce when stirred to anger. This conflict was begun on the timing and terms of others. It will end in a way,

and at an hour, of our choosing.

Our purpose as a nation is firm. Yet our wounds as a people are recent and unhealed, and lead us to pray. In many of our prayers this week, there is a searching, and an honesty. At St. Patrick's Cathedral in New York on Tuesday, a woman said, "I prayed to God to give us a sign that He is still here." Others have prayed for the same, searching hospital to hospital, carrying pictures of those still missing.

God's signs are not always the ones we look for. We learn in tragedy that his purposes are not always our own. Yet the prayers of private suffering, whether in our homes or in this great cathedral, are known and heard, and understood.

There are prayers that help us last through the day, or endure the night. There are prayers of friends and strangers, that give us strength for the journey. And there are prayers that yield our will to a will greater than our own.

This world He created is of moral design. Grief and tragedy and hatred are only for

*US President George W. Bush makes
remarks during the National Day
of Prayer and Remembrance Service
14th September 2001 at the National
Cathedral in Washington, DC.*

*US President George W. Bush (L)
is touched by his father, Former
President George Bush (C) while his
mother Barbara (R) looks on after
making remarks to the Nation during
the National Day of Prayer and
Remembrance Service 14th September,
2001 at the National Cathedral in
Washington, DC. Four former US
Presidents and members of congress
attended the prayer service.*

a time. Goodness, remembrance, and love have no end. And the Lord of life holds all who die, and all who mourn.

It is said that adversity introduces us to ourselves. This is true of a nation as well. In this trial, we have been reminded, and the world has seen, that our fellow Americans are generous and kind, resourceful and brave. We see our national character in rescuers working past exhaustion; in long lines of blood donors; in thousands of citizens who have asked to work and serve in any way possible.

And we have seen our national character in eloquent acts of sacrifice. Inside the World Trade Center, one man who could have saved himself stayed until the end at the side of his quadriplegic friend. A beloved priest died giving the last rites to a firefighter. Two office workers, finding a disabled stranger, carried her down sixty-eight floors to safety. A group of men drove through the night from Dallas to Washington to bring skin grafts for burn victims.

In these acts, and in many others, Americans showed a deep commitment to one another, and an abiding love for our country. Today, we feel what Franklin Roosevelt called the warm courage of national unity. This is a unity of every faith, and every background.

It has joined together political parties in both houses of Congress. It is evident in services of prayer and candlelight vigils, and American flags, which are displayed in pride, and wave in defiance.

Our unity is a kinship of grief, and a steadfast resolve to prevail against our enemies. And this unity against terror is now extending across the world.

America is a nation full of good fortune, with so much to be grateful for. But we are not spared from suffering. In every generation, the world has produced enemies of human freedom. They have attacked America, because we are freedom's home and defender. And the commitment of our fathers is now the calling of our time.

On this national day of prayer and remembrance, we ask almighty God to watch over our nation, and grant us patience and resolve in all that is to come. We pray that He will comfort and console those who now walk in sorrow. We thank Him for each life we now must mourn, and the promise of a life to come.

As we have been assured, neither death nor life, nor angels nor principalities nor powers, nor things present nor things to come, nor height nor depth, can separate us from God's love. May He bless the souls of the departed. May He comfort our own. And may He always guide our country.

God bless America.

People entering St Paul's Cathedral, London, prior to the service in memory of those killed in the US terrorism attacks. Britain's Queen Elizabeth II was expected to lead the nation's tributes to those who died, at a special service at St Paul's Cathedral. 14th September 2001.

The Duke of York, representing the Queen and US ambassador William Farish (left) standing solemnly side-by-side as a military band plays the US national anthem for the first time at a special the Changing of the Guard ceremony at Buckingham Palace. There were a crowd of well-wishers eight deep at the Palace railings that waved flags, clapped and cheered. The two men stared grim-faced ahead as the anthem gave way to a two-minute silence to honour the victims of the atrocities in New York and Washington. This was followed by the British national anthem. Then the band from the outgoing Number 7 Company, Coldstream Guards, played a selection of sombre US music, including Hymn for the Fallen, written by US composer John Williams and used in the final credits of the film, Saving Private Ryan. 14th September 2001.

With the skyline of New York City as a backdrop, people light candles after 7:00 pm 14th September 2001 to remember those lost in the World Trade Center disaster.

A fireman is in a contemplative mood as the skirl of bagpipes broke the still morning air as hundreds of New York City fire-fighters paid last respects to Mychal Judge, their chaplain of 10 years who perished in the destruction of the World Trade Center. Judge, a 68-year-old Franciscan priest, died while giving last rites to a fire-fighter who perished when the twin towers collapsed after two hijacked passenger jets rammed into them. 15th September 2001

People bring photos and pay tribute at the Union Square after the tragedy of World Trade Center collapsing after a terrorist attack. 15th September 2001.

A collection of photographs of those killed (except for 92 victims and terrorists) during the terrorists attacks on September 11, 2001.

Former President Bill Clinton and daughter Chelsea join New York City fire-fighters in paying last respects to Mychal Judge, their chaplain of 10 years who perished in the destruction of the World Trade Center. 15th September 2001.

New York Senator Hillary Clinton meets firemen as the skirl of bagpipes broke the still morning air as hundreds of New York City fire-fighters paid last respects to Mychal Judge, their chaplain of 10 years who perished in the destruction of the World Trade Center. 15th September 2001

Three women hug on the Brooklyn Promenade at sunset 16th September 2001 in New York. The site of the World Trade Center continues to burn in the distance five days after the terrorist attack that destroyed the twin towers of the World Trade Center.

The Mayor of N.Y.C., Rudolph Giuliani attending a service in St Patrick's Cathedral, five days after the terrorist attacks in New York and Washington. 17th September 2001.

US President George W. Bush (3rd R), with Vice President Dick Cheney (4th R), Communications Director Karen Hughs (2nd R) and the White House Staff, have a moment of silence 18th September 2001 at 8:45 am on the South Lawn of the White House in Washington, DC to remember the victims of last weeks terror attacks in New York, Washington, DC, and Pennsylvania.

An American couple mourns near the site of the destroyed World Trade Center, where citizens displayed pictures of missing people near New York's Hudson River, Thursday, 18th September 2001.

"This was the first capital of the United States. All of those...buildings were in the Wall Street area. So in addition to being the financial capital of the United States and the World, Wall Street is a monument to our liberty."

Mayor Rudolph Giuliani

French President Jacques Chirac brings a bouquet of flowers to a memorial in Union Square for the victims of the World Trade Centre attack in New York City. 19th September 2001.

Manuel Rojas (R) comforts his wife Libia (L) as she cries during a prayer vigil in Miami, Florida 18th September, 2001. A week after two commercial airliners were hijacked and flown into the World Trade Center Towers in New York City and the Pentagon, people all around the country mourn for those lost and still missing from the attack.

Students and faculty from The Catholic University of America in Washington, DC, participate in a Vigil of Hope, 18th September 2001, in remembrance of Karen Kincaid, adjunct professor at the Columbus School of Law, and the many others who were lost in the 11th September 2001 terrorist attacks on the Pentagon in Washington and the World Trade Center in New York. Kincaid was a passenger on American Flight 77, which crashed into the Pentagon.

New York police officers carry the coffin of Dominick A. Pezzulo, 33, into a car while a priest gives the last blessing outside St. Michael's church in the Bronx of New York, Wednesday, 19th September 2001. Pezzulo, a police officer with the New York Port Authority, was killed 11th September during the attack and the collapse of the World Trade Center, along with 22 other Police Officers.

New York police officers embrace each other during the funeral service of Dominick A. Pezzulo, 33, outside St. Michael's church in the Bronx of New York, Wednesday, 19th September 2001. Pezzulo, a police officer with the New York Port Authority, was killed 11th September during the attack and the collapse of the World Trade Center.

German Foreign Minister Joschka Fischer (L) pays his respect to the 15 fireman of the ninth battalion of the New York fire brigade "Engine 54", who lost their lives in the 11 September terrorist attack on the World Trade Center, as he arrives for a short visit to the battalion in Manhattan, Thursday 20th September 2001.

New York City Mayor Rudolph Giuliani (R) is surrounded by religious leaders from New York as he speaks to the crowd at "A Prayer For America" memorial service at New York's Yankee Stadium 23rd September 2001 to remember the victims of the 11th September World Trade Center attack. The service is aimed at sending a message of hope.

Wearing a hard hat for her work at the site of the World Trade Center attacks, a New York Police officer looks at photographs of missing police members and fire-fighters at a makeshift memorial, 26th September 2001 in New York.

CITYWIDE PRAYER SERVICE AT YANKEE
STADIUM
MAYOR RUDY GIULIANI - SEPTEMBER 23RD

"On September 11th, New York City suffered the darkest day in our history. It is now up to us to make this our finest hour.

"Today we come together in the Capital of the World, as a united City. We're accompanied by religious leaders of every faith, to offer a prayer for the families of those who have been lost...to offer a prayer for our City... and to offer a prayer for America.

"The proud Twin Towers that once crowned our famous skyline -- no longer stand. But our skyline will rise again.

"In the words of President George W. Bush, 'we will rebuild New York City.'

"To those who say that our City will never be the same, I say you are right. It will be better.

"Now we understand much more clearly why people from all over the globe want to come to New York, and to America... why they always have, and why they always will.

"It's called freedom, equal protection under law, respect for human life, and the promise of opportunity.

"All of the victims of this tragedy were innocent.

"All of them were heroes.

"The Bible says [John 15:13] 'Greater love hath no man than this, that a man lay down his life for his friends.' Our brave New York City Firefighters . . . New York City Police Officers . . . Port Authority Police Officers . . . EMS workers . . . health care workers . . . court officers . . . and uniformed service members . . .

"They laid down their lives for strangers. They were inspired by their sense of duty and their love for humanity. As they raced into the Twin Towers and the other buildings to save lives, they didn't stop to ask how rich or poor the person was, they didn't stop to ask what religion, what race, what nationality. They just raced in to save their fellow human beings.

"They are the best example of love that we have in our society.

"The people they were trying to rescue – the people who worked in the World Trade Center and the buildings around it – were each engaged in the quiet heroism of supporting their families, pursuing their dreams and playing their own meaningful part in a diverse, dynamic and free society. They represented more than 60 different nations. They will also occupy a permanent and sacred place in our history and in our hearts.

"Even in the midst of the darkest tragedy there are miracles that help our faith to go on. I would like to share one miracle of September 11th with you.

"St. Paul's Chapel is one of the oldest and most historic buildings in the City of New York. It was built in 1766, when the surrounding area was still countryside. The Chapel survived our war of independence -- including seven years of wartime occupation.

"After George Washington was inaugurated the first President of the United States, in New York City on April 30th, 1789, he walked to St. Paul's, and he kneeled down to pray. The pew where he worshipped is still there. Framed on the wall beside it is the oldest known representation of the Great Seal of the United States of America -- it's a majestic eagle, holding in one talon an olive branch, proclaiming our abiding desire for peace . . . and in the other, a cluster of arrows, a forewarning of our determination to defend our liberty. On a banner above the Eagle is written E Pluribus Unum, 'Out of Many, One.'

"For the past 25 years, the chapel stood directly in the shadow of the World Trade Center Towers. When the Towers fell, more than a dozen modern buildings were destroyed and damaged. Yet somehow, amid all the destruction and devastation, St. Paul's Chapel still stands . . . without so much as a broken window.

"It's a small miracle in some ways, but the presence of that chapel standing defiant and serene amid the ruins of war sends an eloquent message about the strength and resilience of the people of New York City, and the people of America.

"We unite under the banner of E Pluribus Unum. We find strength in our diversity. We're a city where people look different, talk different, think different. But we're a City at one with all of the people at the World Trade Center, and with all of America. We love our diversity, and we love our freedom.

"Like our founding fathers who fought and died for freedom . . . like our ancestors who fought and died to preserve our union and to end the sin of slavery . . . like our fathers and grandfathers who fought and died to liberate the world from Nazism, and Fascism, and Communism . . . the cluster of arrows to defend our freedom, and the olive branch of peace have now been handed to us.

"We will hold them firmly in our hands, honor their memory, and lift them up toward heaven to light the world.

"In the days since this attack, we have met the worst of humanity with the best of humanity.

"We pray for our President, George W. Bush . . . and for our Governor George Pataki . . . who have provided us with such inspiring leadership during these very, very difficult times. We pray for all of those whose loved ones are lost or missing . . . we pray for our children, and we say to them: 'Do not be afraid. It's safe to live your life.' Finally, we pray for America . . . and for all of those who join us in defending freedom, law, and humanity.

"We humbly bow our heads and we ask God to bless the City of New York, and we ask God to bless the United States of America.

"Thank you."

A New York City Fire Truck carrying the casket of Captain Terence Hatton of the NYFD down Fifth Avenue for a service at St. Patrick's Cathedral 4th October 2001. Hatton, who was 41, was killed in the 11 September attack on the World Trade Center. A total of 343 Firefighters perished.

US President George W. Bush wipes his nose, at the start of the 20th Annual National Fallen Fighters Memorial Tribute 7th October 2001 at the National Fire Academy in Emmitsburg, Maryland. The President delivered remarks for the 101 fire-fighters from across the US who died in the line of duty in 2000. The names of the fallen fire fighters killed in the terrorist attack on the World Trade Center will be added next year.

One month after the terrorist attacks on the World Trade Center, workers pause to watch a memorial service through broken windows of a damaged pedestrian bridge 11th October, 2001, at the site of the ruins of the twin 110-story towers in New York. A short ceremony marking the attack was held at ground zero of the ruins.

Rescue workers search through the wreckage of the World Trade Center, 24th September 2001, in New York. Declaring that a "miracle" was needed to find anyone alive in the ruins of the World Trade Center, Mayor Rudolph Giuliani said today he would simplify procedures to issue death certificates, and rescue workers admitted they wanted closure

US President George W. Bush waves a flag while singing "The Battle Hymn Of The Republic" during a memorial service at the Pentagon in Washington, DC 11th October 2001, marking the one-month anniversary of the terrorist hijacks which crashed four commercial airplanes in New York, Pennsylvania and into the Pentagon. One hundred eighty nine people died at the Pentagon in that crash.

A British War veteran takes part in a remembrance service at the War Memorial in York. Along with the traditional poppy and medals is a US flag to remember victims of the September terrorist attacks in New York and Washington. 9th November 2001.

US Vice President Dick Cheney (L) speaks to the media as he stands at ground zero of the World Trade Center ruins in New York. New York Governor George Pataki (C) and New York City Mayor Rudolph Giuliani (R) gave Cheney a tour of the site. 18th October 2001.

A flag flies at Ground Zero as work continues on the site of the former World Trade Center on Friday, 9th November 2001, in New York. Almost two months after the terrorist attack which destroyed the twin World Trade Center towers the ruins emit acrid fumes while fires trapped underground rise to the surface every day as contractors work to clear the area of some two million tons of rubble.

The chief of the service of voluntary workers of Padua's civil defence, Renato Lambini (L), gives an Italian flag as a present to the commander of New York City fire-fighters, Daniel Nigro, on a stage in Piazza del Popolo, in downtown Rome, on Saturday 10th November 2001 during the rally for the US-Day organized by ruling "House for Freedoms" centre-right coalition to support the United States after the 11th September's terrorist attacks against New York and Washington. The cardboard wall on the background, under the Italian and US flags, reads the words "Per non dimenticare" (To not forget).

The Union Jack flag, left, carried by Detective Constable Ron Cuthbertson and the American flag carried by Lieutenant Amy Monroe from the New York Fire Department, are received by the Dean of Westminster, Wesley Carr, centre, ... in London's Westminster Abbey at the beginning of a service for the British victims of the terrorist attacks on the United States. 29th November 2001.

Britain's Queen Elizabeth II, accompanied by the Prince of Wales, about to lay a wreath on the Rememberance Stone outside Westminster Abbey in London. Following a memorial service to those who died in the September 11th terrorist attacks in New York. 29th November 2001.

New York City Fire-fighters, police officers and construction crews gather for a memorial service at ground zero to mark the three month anniversary of the attacks on the World Trade Center 11th December 2001 in New York City.

REMARKS BY THE PRESIDENT AT THE WORLD WILL ALWAYS REMEMBER SEPTEMBER 11TH CEREMONY

THE PRESIDENT: A great writer has said that the struggle of humanity against tyranny is the struggle of memory against forgetting. When we fight terror, we fight tyranny; and so we remember. We remember the perfect blueness of the sky that Tuesday morning. We remember the children traveling without their mothers when their planes were hijacked.

We remember the cruelty of the murderers and the pain and anguish of the murdered. Every one of the innocents who died on September the 11th was the most important person on earth to somebody. Every death extinguished a world.

We remember the courage of the rescue workers and the outpouring of friendship and sympathy from nations around the world. We remember how we felt that day: our sadness, the surge of love for our country, our anger, and our determination to right this huge wrong.

Today, the wrong is being righted and justice is being done. We still have far to go. And many dangers lie ahead. Yet, there can be no doubt how this conflict will end. Our enemies have made the mistake that America's enemies always make. They saw liberty and thought they saw weakness. And now, they see defeat.

In time, this war will end. But our remembrance never will. All around this beautiful city are statues of our heroes, memorials, museums and archives that preserve our national experience, our achievements and our failures, our defeats and our victories.

This republic is young, but its memory is long. Now, we have inscribed a new memory alongside those others. It's a memory of tragedy and shock, of loss and mourning. But not only of loss and mourning. It's also a memory of bravery and self-sacrifice, and the love that lays down its life for a friend -- even a friend whose name it never knew.

We are privileged to have with us the families of many of the heroes on September the 11th, including the family of Jeremy Glick of Flight 93. His courage and self-sacrifice may have saved the White House. It is right and fitting that it is here we pay our respects.

In time, perhaps, we will mark the memory of September the 11th in stone and metal — something we can show children as yet unborn to help them understand what happened on this minute and on this day. But for those of us who lived through these events, the only marker we'll ever need is the tick of a clock at the 46th minute of the eighth hour of the 11th day. We will remember where we were and how we felt. We will remember the dead and what we owe them. We will remember what we lost and what we found.

And in our time, we will honor the memory of the 11th day by doing our duty as citizens of this great country, freedom's home and freedoms defender. God bless.

A group of bagpipers play at the conclusion of a memorial service at ground zero to mark the three month anniversary of the attacks on the World Trade Center, 11th December 2001, in New York City.

REMARKS BY THE PRESIDENT ON THE SIX-MONTH ANNIVERSARY OF THE SEPTEMBER 11TH ATTACKS

THE PRESIDENT: Diplomatic representatives of the coalition of nations; members of the Congress, the Cabinet, the Supreme Court; members of the American Armed Forces; military coalition members from around the world; distinguished guests; and ladies and gentlemen. Welcome to the White House.

We have come together to mark a terrible day, to reaffirm a just and vital cause, and to thank the many nations that share our resolve and will share our common victory.

Six months separate us from September the 11th. Yet, for the families of the lost, each day brings new pain; each day requires new courage. Your grace and strength have been an example to our nation. America will not forget the lives that were taken, and the justice their death requires.

We face an enemy of ruthless ambition, unconstrained by law or morality. The terrorists despise other religions and have defiled their own. And they are determined to expand the scale and scope of their murder. The terror that targeted New York and Washington could next strike any center of civilization. Against such an enemy, there is no immunity, and there can be no neutrality.

Many nations and many families have lived in the shadows of terrorism for decades -- enduring years of mindless and merciless killing. September the 11th was not the beginning of global terror, but it was the beginning of the world's concerted response. History will know that day not only as a day of tragedy, but as a day of decision -- when the civilized world was stirred to anger and to action. And the terrorists will remember September 11th as the day their reckoning began.

A mighty coalition of civilized nations is now defending our common security. Terrorist assets have been frozen.

Terrorist front groups have been exposed. A terrorist regime has been toppled from power. Terrorist plots have been unraveled, from Spain to Singapore. And thousands of terrorists have been brought to justice, are in prison, or are running in fear of their lives.

With us today are representatives from many of our partners in this great work, and we're proud to display their flags at the White House this morning. From the contributions these nations have made -- some well known, others not -- I am honored to extend the deepest gratitude of the people of the United States.

The power and vitality of our coalition have been proven in Afghanistan. More than half of the forces now assisting the heroic Afghan fighters, or providing security in Kabul, are from countries other than the United States. There are many examples of commitment: our good ally, France, has deployed nearly one-fourth of its navy to support Operation Enduring Freedom, and Great Britain has sent its largest naval task force in 20 years. British and American special operations forces have fought beside teams from Australia, and Canada, Norway, Denmark and Germany. In total, 17 nations have forces deployed in the region. And we could not have done our work without critical support from countries, particularly like Pakistan and Uzbekistan.

Japanese destroyers are refueling coalition ships in the Indian Ocean. The Turkish air force has refueled American planes. Afghans are receiving treatment in hospitals built by Russians, Jordanians, Spanish, and have received supplies and help from South Korea.

Nations in our coalition have shared in the responsibilities and sacrifices of our cause. On the day before September the 11th, I met with Prime Minister John Howard of Australia, who spoke of the common beliefs and shared affection of our two countries. We could not have known that bond was about to be proven again in war, and we could not have known its human cost. Last month, Sergeant Andrew Russell of the Australian Special Air Service, died in Afghanistan. He left behind his wife, Kylie, and their daughter,

Leisa, just 11 days old. Friends said of Sergeant Russell, "You could rely on him never to let you down."

This young man, and many like him, have not let us down. Each life taken from us is a terrible loss. We have lost young people from Germany, and Denmark, and Afghanistan, and America. We mourn each one. And for their bravery in a noble cause, we honor them.

Part of that cause was to liberate the Afghan people from terrorist occupation, and we did so. Next week, the schools reopen in Afghanistan. They will be open to all -- and many young girls will go to school for the first time in their young lives. Afghanistan has many difficult challenges ahead -- and, yet, we've averted mass starvation, begun clearing mine fields, rebuilding roads and improving health care. In Kabul, a friendly government is now an essential member of the coalition against terror.

Now that the Taliban are gone and al Qaeda has lost its home base for terrorism, we have entered the second stage of the war on terror -- a sustained campaign to deny sanctuary to terrorists who would threaten our citizens from anywhere in the world.

In Afghanistan, hundreds of trained killers are now dead. Many have been captured. Others are still on the run, hoping to strike again. These terrorist fighters are the most committed, the most dangerous, and the least likely to surrender. They are trying to regroup, and we'll stop them. For five months in Afghanistan, our coalition has been patient and relentless. And more patience and more courage will be required. We're fighting a fierce battle in the Shah-i-kot Mountains, and we're winning. Yet, it will not be the last battle in Afghanistan. And there will be other battles beyond that nation.

For terrorists fleeing Afghanistan -- for any terrorist looking for a base of operations, there must be no refuge, no safe haven. By driving terrorists from place to place, we disrupt the planning and training for further attacks on America and the civilized world. Every terrorist must be made to live as an international fugitive, with no place to settle or organize, no place to hide, no governments to hide behind, and not even a safe place to sleep.

I have set a clear policy in the second stage of the war on terror: America encourages and expects governments everywhere to help remove the terrorist parasites that threaten their own countries and peace of the world. If governments need training, or resources to meet this commitment, America will help.

We are helping right now in the Philippines, where terrorists with links to al Qaeda are trying to seize the southern part of the country to establish a militant regime. They are oppressing local peoples, and have kidnapped both American and Filipino citizens. America has sent more than 500 troops to train Philippine forces. We stand with President Arroyo, who is courageously opposing the threat of terror.

In the Republic of Georgia, terrorists working closely with al Qaeda operate in the Pankisi Gorge near the Russian border. At President Shevardnadze's request, the United States is planning to send up to 150 military trainers to prepare Georgian soldiers to reestablish control in this lawless region. This temporary assistance serves the interests of both our countries.

In Yemen, we are working to avert the possibility of another Afghanistan. Many al Qaeda recruits come from near the Yemen-Saudi Arabian border, and al Qaeda may try to reconstitute itself in remote corners of that region. President Saleh has assured me that he is committed to confronting this danger. We will help Yemeni forces with both training and equipment to prevent that land from becoming a haven for terrorists.

In the current stage of the war, our coalition is opposing not a nation, but a network. Victory will come over time, as that network is patiently and steadily dismantled. This will require international cooperation on a number of fronts: diplomatic, financial and military. We will not send American troops to every battle, but America will actively prepare other nations for the battles ahead. This mission will end when the

work is finished -- when terror networks of global reach have been defeated. The havens and training camps of terror are a threat to our lives and to our way of life, and they will be destroyed.

At the same time, every nation in our coalition must take seriously the growing threat of terror on a catastrophic scale -- terror armed with biological, chemical, or nuclear weapons. America is now consulting with friends and allies about this greatest of dangers, and we're determined to confront it.

Here is what we already know: some states that sponsor terror are seeking or already possess weapons of mass destruction; terrorist groups are hungry for these weapons, and would use them without a hint of conscience. And we know that these weapons, in the hands of terrorists, would unleash blackmail and genocide and chaos.

These facts cannot be denied, and must be confronted. In preventing the spread of weapons of mass destruction, there is no margin for error, and no chance to learn from mistakes. Our coalition must act deliberately, but inaction is not an option. Men with no respect for life must never be allowed to control the ultimate instruments of death.

Gathered here today, we are six months along -- a short time in a long struggle. And our war on terror will be judged by its finish, not by its start. More dangers and sacrifices lie ahead. Yet, America is prepared. Our resolve has only grown, because we remember. We remember the horror and heroism of that morning -- the death of children on a field trip, the resistance of passengers on a doomed airplane, the courage of rescuers who died with strangers they were trying to save. And we remember the video images of terrorists who laughed at our loss.

Every civilized nation has a part in this struggle, because every civilized nation has a stake in its outcome. There can be no peace in a world where differences and grievances become an excuse to target the innocent for murder. In fighting terror, we fight for the conditions that will make lasting peace possible. We fight for

lawful change against chaotic violence, for human choice against coercion and cruelty, and for the dignity and goodness of every life.

Every nation should know that, for America, the war on terror is not just a policy, it's a pledge. I will not relent in this struggle for the freedom and security of my country and the civilized world.

And we'll succeed.

There will be a day when the organized threat against America, our friends and allies is broken. And when the terrorists are disrupted and scattered and discredited, many old conflicts will appear in a new light -- without the constant fear and cycle of bitterness that terrorists spread with their violence. We will see then that the old and serious disputes can be settled within the bounds of reason, and goodwill, and mutualsecurity. I see a peaceful world beyond the war on terror, and with courage and unity, we are building that world together.

Any nation that makes an unequivocal commitment against terror can join this cause. Every nation of goodwill is welcome. And, together, we will face the peril of our moment, and seize the promise of our times.

May God bless our coalition.

President George W. Bush (C) delivers a speech at ceremonies commemorating the six-month anniversary of the 11th September 2001 terrorist attacks against the US, on the South Lawn at the White House 11th March 2002 in Washington, DC.(previous pages)

A New York City fire-fighter looks up at a makeshift cross made from steel at Ground Zero during a prayer service 11th March 2001 at 8:46 am to commemorate the six-month anniversary of the attack on the World Trade Center. A moment in silence was held all over the city to mark the moment the first of two hijacked airliners struck the Twin Towers.

A statue depicting iron workers taking a break on a beam sits near the viewing stand near Ground Zero in New York, NY, 7th March 2002. Six months after the twin towers of World Trade Center crumbled in terrorist attacks, they will be reborn by the magic of two giant beams of light that will pierce the sky over Manhattan.

The President

President George W. Bush's early morning school reading event in Sarasota, Florida, is interrupted by his chief of staff Andrew Card (left) shortly after news of the New York City airplane crashes was available.

President Bush leads the students and teachers of Emma E. Booker Elementary School in Sarasota, Florida, in a moment of silence shortly after hearing about the plane crashes in New York City.

STATEMENT BY THE PRESIDENT
IN HIS ADDRESS TO THE NATION
SEPTEMBER 11, 2001

THE PRESIDENT: Good evening. Today, our fellow citizens, our way of life, our very freedom came under attack in a series of deliberate and deadly terrorist acts. The victims were in airplanes, or in their offices; secretaries, businessmen and women, military and federal workers; moms and dads, friends and neighbors. Thousands of lives were suddenly ended by evil, despicable acts of terror.

The pictures of airplanes flying into buildings, fires burning, huge structures collapsing, have filled us with disbelief, terrible sadness, and a quiet, unyielding anger. These acts of mass murder were intended to frighten our nation into chaos and retreat. But they have failed; our country is strong.

A great people has been moved to defend a great nation. Terrorist attacks can shake the foundations of our biggest buildings, but they cannot touch the foundation of America. These acts shattered steel, but they cannot dent the steel of American resolve.

America was targeted for attack because we're the brightest beacon for freedom and opportunity in the world. And no one will keep that light from shining.

Today, our nation saw evil, the very worst of human nature. And we responded with the best of America—with the daring of our rescue workers, with the caring for strangers and neighbors who came to give blood and help in any way they could.

Immediately following the first attack, I implemented our government's emergency response plans. Our military is powerful, and it's prepared. Our emergency teams are working in New York City and Washington, D.C., to help with local rescue efforts.

Our first priority is to get help to those who have been injured, and to take every precaution to protect our citizens at home and around the world from further attacks.

The functions of our government continue without interruption. Federal agencies in Washington, which had to be evacuated today, are reopening for essential personnel tonight, and will be open for business tomorrow. Our financial institutions remain strong, and the American economy will be open for business, as well.

The search is under way for those who are behind these evil acts. I've directed the full resources of our intelligence and law enforcement communities to find those responsible and to bring them to justice. We will make no distinction between the terrorists who committed these acts and those who harbor them.

I appreciate so very much the members of Congress who have joined me in strongly condemning these attacks. And on behalf of the American people, I thank the many world leaders who have called to offer their condolences and assistance.

America and our friends and allies join with all those who want peace and security in the world, and we stand together to win the war against terrorism. Tonight, I ask for your prayers for all those who grieve, for the children whose worlds have been shattered, for all whose sense of safety and security has been threatened. And I pray they will be comforted by a power greater than any of us, spoken through the ages in Psalm 23: "Even though I walk through the valley of the shadow of death, I fear no evil, for You are with me."

This is a day when all Americans from every walk of life unite in our resolve for justice and peace. America has stood down enemies before, and we will do so this time. None of us will ever forget this day. Yet, we go forward to defend freedom and all that is good and just in our world. Thank you. Good night, and God bless America.

President Bush talks on the phone with New York Mayor Rudy Giuliani and New York Governor George Pataki aboard Air Force One. Bush gave a statement about the two planes that crashed into the World Trade Center and one that crashed into the Pentagon earlier on September 11.

President Bush addresses the nation from the Oval Office on September 11, 2001, at the White House in Washington, D.C.

President Bush steps off Air Force One at Barksdale Air Force Base in Shreveport, Louisiana, on September 11 after leaving Sarasota, Florida.

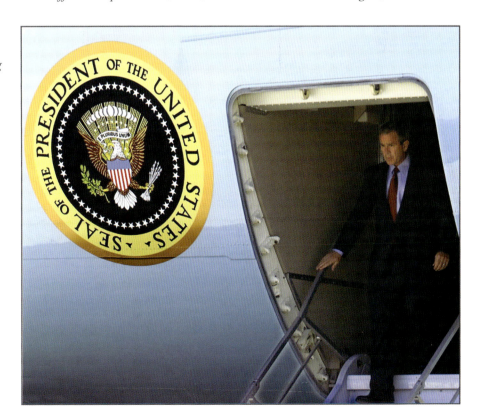

President Bush addresses the nation and the world from Barksdale AFB in Shreveport.

President Bush greets the servicemen and women of a specialized unit assisting in recovery operations at the damaged Pentagon as he tours the impact area at the Pentagon where a hijacked airline was crashed into the building as part of a coordinated terrorist attack.

President Bush (center), Vice President Dick Cheney (second from right), and Chairman of the Joint Chiefs of Staff General Henry H. Shelton (right) prepare for a National Security team meeting as Secretary of Defense Donald Rumsfeld (left) and Secretary of State Colin Powell (second from left) confer on September 12 in the Cabinet Room of the White House.

President Bush (center) watches the arrival of the color guard during the National Day of Prayer and Remembrance Service on September 14 at the National Cathedral in Washington, D.C. Members of Congress and four former U.S. presidents attended the prayer service.

In this photo released by the White House, President Bush (center) speaks to his National Security Council team during a meeting in the Cabinet Room of the White House, one day after terrorist attacks in New York and Washington. Left to right are Secretary of Defense Donald Rumsfeld, Secretary of State Colin Powell, Bush, Vice President Dick Cheney, and Chairman of the Joint Chiefs of Staff Henry Shelton.

President Bush stands in the Oval Office after making a phone call to New York City Mayor Rudolph Giuliani and New York Governor George Pataki on September 13, in the aftermath of the terrorist attacks. Bush told the media gathered, "I am also someone however who's got a job to do, and I intend to do it. And this is a terrible moment." Secretary of State Powell confirmed in a press conference on September 13 in Washington that exiled Saudi dissident Osama bin Laden is a main suspect in the terrorist attacks. Powell said that recent U.S. diplomatic overtures to Pakistan were aimed at securing Islamabad's cooperation in dealing with bin Laden, who lives in neighboring Afghanistan.

PRESIDENT BUSH SALUTES HEROES IN NEW YORK, SEPTEMBER 14, 2001

CROWD: U.S.A.! U.S.A.!

THE PRESIDENT: Thank you all. I want you all to know—

Q: Can't hear you.

THE PRESIDENT: I can't talk any louder. (Laughter.)

I want you all to know that America today—that America today is on bended knee in prayer for the people whose lives were lost here, for the workers who work here, for the families who mourn. This nation stands with the good people of New York City, and New Jersey and Connecticut, as we mourn the loss of thousands of our citizens.

Q: I can't hear you.

THE PRESIDENT: I can hear you. (Applause.)

I can hear you. The rest of the world hears you. (Applause.) And the people who knocked these buildings down will hear all of us soon. (Applause.)

CROWD: U.S.A.! U.S.A.!

THE PRESIDENT: The nation sends its love and compassion to everybody who is here. Thank you for your hard work. Thank you for making the nation proud. And may God bless America. (Applause.)

CROWD: U.S.A.! U.S.A.!

President Bush talks with the media and resting Los Angeles firefighters beside New York City Mayor Rudy Giuliani (left) and New York Governor George Pataki (center, rear) on September 14, as Bush tours the catastrophic damage to the World Trade Center.

President Bush delivers an opening statement on September 15, prior to a meeting with his National Security team at Camp David, the presidential retreat in Maryland. Bush said that he is committed to finding the terrorists who perpetrated the attacks in New York City and Washington, and that all U.S. uniformed personnel must be at the ready. Bush holds the badge of Port Authority Police Officer George Howard.

REMARKS BY THE PRESIDENT UPON
ARRIVAL AT THE WHITE HOUSE

THE PRESIDENT: Today, millions of Americans mourned and prayed, and tomorrow we go back to work. Today, people from all walks of life gave thanks for the heroes; they mourn the dead; they ask for God's good graces on the families who mourn, and tomorrow the good people of America go back to their shops, their fields, American factories, and go back to work.

Our nation was horrified, but it's not going to be terrorized. We're a great nation. We're a nation of resolve. We're a nation that can't be cowed by evil-doers. I've got great faith in the American people. If the American people had seen what I had seen in New York City, you'd have great faith, too. You'd have faith in the hard work of the rescuers; you'd have great faith because of the desire for people to do what's right for America; you'd have great faith because of the compassion and love that our fellow Americans are showing each other in times of need.

I also have faith in our military. And we have got a job to do—just like the farmers and ranchers and business owners and factory workers have a job to do. My administration has a job to do, and we're going to do it. We will rid the world of the evil-doers. We will call together freedom loving people to fight terrorism.

And on this day of—on the Lord's Day, I say to my fellow Americans, thank you for your prayers, thank you for your compassion, thank you for your love for one another. And tomorrow when you get back to work, work hard like you always have. But we've been warned. We've been warned there are evil people in this world. We've been warned so vividly—and we'll be alert. Your government is alert. The governors and mayors are alert that evil folks still lurk out there.

As I said yesterday, people have declared war on America, and they have made a terrible mistake, because this is a fabulous country. Our economy will come back. We'll still be the best farmers and ranchers in the world. We're still the most innovative entrepreneurs in the world. On this day of faith, I've never had more faith in America than I have right now.

President Bush speaks on his return to the White House on September 16 after a weekend of high level talks with top members of his cabinet and security council at the presidential retreat of Camp David.

President Bush pounds his fist during a press conference while meeting with military leaders at the Pentagon on September 17. Bush said that the United States wants Saudi-born suspected terrorism mastermind Osama bin Laden brought to justice "dead or alive."

This photo released by the White House shows President Bush (center) meeting with Transportation Secretary Norman Mineta (left), Deputy Chief of Staff Josh Bolten (second from right), and White House Counsel Al Gonzalez in the Roosevelt Room of the White House to discuss the airline industry in the wake of the September 11 terrorist attacks with hijacked commercial jets. Mineta is expected to meet with airline executives on September 18 to discuss government aid for the industry.

President Bush meets with Islamic community and religious leaders during a tour of the Islamic Center in Washington, D.C., on September 17.

President Bush answers questions from the media as National Security Adviser Condoleezza Rice (left) and Secretary of Defense Donald Rumsfeld (right) look on during a meeting with military leaders at the Pentagon on September 17.

REMARKS BY THE PRESIDENT WITH HOUSE AND SENATE LEADERSHIP

THE PRESIDENT: I want to welcome the members of the leadership of the Congress here, and I want the nation to know how proud I am of how they have helped unite our country. Senator Daschle and the Speaker and Senator Lott and Representative Gephardt have really showed that in times of emergency and crisis, that our government can function in a way that is just exemplary. And I want to thank them for coming down.

I'm also so pleased to accept the invitation of the Speaker and the leaders to come and address the Congress tomorrow night. I look forward to the opportunity to explain to the American people who it is and who would do this to our great country, and why—why would people choose America?

A lot of our citizens have got a lot of questions about what has taken place on September the 11th and subsequent to that. And I owe it to the country to give an explanation. And I want to thank the Congress for giving me a chance. I can't think of a better place to talk about freedom and the battle to maintain freedom in one of the greatest halls of freedom. And that is in the United States Congress.

So, thank you for the invitation. I accept wholeheartedly, and I will see you all tomorrow night.

Members of Congress applaud President Bush September 20 as he addresses a joint session of the Congress on Capitol Hill in Washington, D.C. Bush called the joint session to explain his position on the U.S. reaction to the September 11 terrorist strikes.

ADDRESS TO A JOINT SESSION OF CONGRESS AND THE AMERICAN PEOPLE, UNITED STATES CAPITOL, WASHINGTON, D.C.

THE PRESIDENT: Mr. Speaker, Mr. President Pro Tempore, members of Congress, and fellow Americans:

In the normal course of events, Presidents come to this chamber to report on the state of the Union. Tonight, no such report is needed. It has already been delivered by the American people.

We have seen it in the courage of passengers, who rushed terrorists to save others on the ground—passengers like an exceptional man named Todd Beamer. And would you please help me to welcome his wife, Lisa Beamer, here tonight.

We have seen the state of our Union in the endurance of rescuers, working past exhaustion. We have seen the unfurling of flags, the lighting of candles, the giving of blood, the saying of prayers—in English, Hebrew, and Arabic. We have seen the decency of a loving and giving people who have made the grief of strangers their own.

My fellow citizens, for the last nine days, the entire world has seen for itself the state of our Union—and it is strong.

Tonight we are a country awakened to danger and called to defend freedom. Our grief has turned to anger, and anger to resolution. Whether we bring our enemies to justice, or bring justice to our enemies, justice will be done.

I thank the Congress for its leadership at such an important time. All of America was touched on the evening of the tragedy to see Republicans and Democrats joined together on the steps of this Capitol, singing "God Bless America." And you did more than sing; you acted, by delivering $40 billion to rebuild our communities and meet the needs of our military.

Speaker Hastert, Minority Leader Gephardt, Majority Leader Daschle and Senator Lott, I thank you for your friendship, for your leadership, and for your service to our country.

And on behalf of the American people, I thank the world for its outpouring of support. America will never forget the sounds of our National Anthem playing at Buckingham Palace, on the streets of Paris, and at Berlin's Brandenburg Gate.

We will not forget South Korean children gathering to pray outside our embassy in Seoul, or the prayers of sympathy offered at a mosque in Cairo. We will not forget moments of silence and days of mourning in Australia and Africa and Latin America. Nor will we forget the citizens of 80 other nations who died with our own: dozens of Pakistanis; more than 130 Israelis; more than 250 citizens of India; men and women from El Salvador, Iran, Mexico and Japan; and hundreds of British citizens. America has no truer friend than Great Britain. Once again, we are joined together in a great cause—so honored the British Prime Minister has crossed an ocean to show his unity of purpose with America. Thank you for coming, friend.

On September the 11th, enemies of freedom committed an act of war against our country. Americans have known wars—but for the past 136 years, they have been wars on foreign soil, except for one Sunday in 1941. Americans have known the casualties of war—but not at the center of a great city on a peaceful morning. Americans have known surprise attacks—but never before on thousands of civilians. All of this was brought upon us in a single day—and night fell on a different world, a world where freedom itself is under attack.

Americans have many questions tonight. Americans are asking: Who attacked our country? The evidence we have gathered all points to a collection of loosely affiliated terrorist organizations known as al Qaeda. They are the same murderers indicted for bombing American embassies in Tanzania and Kenya, and responsible for bombing the USS Cole.

Al Qaeda is to terror what the mafia is to crime. But its goal is not making money; its goal is remaking the world—and imposing its radical beliefs on people everywhere.

The terrorists practice a fringe form of Islamic extremism that has been rejected by Muslim scholars and the vast majority of Muslim clerics—a fringe movement that perverts the peaceful teachings of Islam. The terrorists' directive commands them to kill Christians and Jews, to kill all Americans, and make no distinction among military and civilians, including women and children.

This group and its leader—a person named Osama bin Laden—are linked to many other organizations in different countries, including the Egyptian Islamic Jihad and the Islamic Movement of Uzbekistan. There are thousands of these terrorists in more than 60 countries. They are recruited from their own nations and neighborhoods and brought to camps in places like Afghanistan, where they are trained in the tactics of terror. They are sent back to their homes or sent to hide in countries around the world to plot evil and destruction.

The leadership of al Qaeda has great influence in Afghanistan and supports the Taliban regime in controlling most of that country. In Afghanistan, we see al Qaeda's vision for the world.

Afghanistan's people have been brutalized—many are starving and many have fled. Women are not allowed to attend school. You can be jailed for owning a television. Religion can be practiced only as their leaders dictate. A man can be jailed in Afghanistan if his beard is not long enough.

The United States respects the people of Afghanistan—after all, we are currently its largest source of humanitarian aid—but we condemn the Taliban regime. It is not only repressing its own people, it is threatening people everywhere by sponsoring and sheltering and supplying terrorists. By aiding and abetting murder, the Taliban regime is committing murder. And tonight, the United States of America makes the following demands on the Taliban: Deliver to United States authorities all the leaders of al Qaeda who hide in your land. Release all foreign nationals, including American citizens, you have unjustly imprisoned. Protect foreign journalists, diplomats, and aid workers in your country. Close immediately and permanently every terrorist training camp in Afghanistan, and hand over every terrorist, and every person in their support structure, to appropriate authorities. Give the United States full access to terrorist training camps, so we can make sure they are no longer operating.

These demands are not open to negotiation or discussion. The Taliban must act, and act immediately. They will hand over the terrorists, or they will share in their fate.

I also want to speak tonight directly to Muslims throughout the world. We respect your faith. It's practiced freely by many millions of Americans, and by millions more in countries that America counts as friends. Its teachings are good and peaceful, and those who commit evil in the name of Allah blaspheme the name of Allah. The terrorists are traitors to their own faith, trying, in effect, to hijack Islam itself. The enemy of America is not our many Muslim friends; it is not our many Arab friends. Our enemy is a radical network of terrorists, and every government that supports them.

Our war on terror begins with al Qaeda, but it does not end there. It will not end until every terrorist group of global reach has been found, stopped and defeated.

Americans are asking: Why do they hate us? They hate what we see right here in this chamber—a democratically elected government. Their leaders are self-appointed. They hate our freedoms—our freedom of religion, our freedom of speech, our freedom to vote and assemble and disagree with each other.

They want to overthrow existing governments in many Muslim countries, such as Egypt, Saudi Arabia, and Jordan. They want to drive Israel out of the Middle East. They want to drive Christians and Jews out of vast regions of Asia and Africa.

These terrorists kill not merely to end lives, but to disrupt and end a way of life. With every atrocity, they hope that America grows fearful, retreating from the world and forsaking our friends. They stand against us, because we stand in their way.

We are not deceived by their pretenses to piety. We have seen their kind before. They are the heirs of all the murderous ideologies of the 20th century. By sacrificing human life to serve their radical visions—by abandoning every value except the will to power—they follow in the path of fascism, and Nazism, and totalitarianism. And they will follow that path all the way, to where it ends: in history's unmarked grave of discarded lies.

Americans are asking: How will we fight and win this war? We will direct every resource at our command—every means of diplomacy, every tool of intelligence, every instrument of law enforcement, every financial influence, and every necessary weapon of war—to the disruption and to the defeat of the global terror network.

This war will not be like the war against Iraq a decade ago, with a decisive liberation of territory and a swift conclusion. It will not look like the air war above Kosovo two years ago, where no ground troops were used and not a single American was lost in combat.

Our response involves far more than instant retaliation and isolated strikes.

President Bush acknowledges the Congress late September 20. Bush addressed a Congressional joint session on Capitol Hill and vowed to use "every resource" to combat global terrorism.

distinguished American to lead this effort, to strengthen American security: a military veteran, an effective governor, a true patriot, a trusted friend—Pennsylvania's Tom Ridge. He will lead, oversee and coordinate a comprehensive national strategy to safeguard our country against terrorism, and respond to any attacks that may come.

These measures are essential. But the only way to defeat terrorism as a threat to our way of life is to stop it, eliminate it, and destroy it where it grows.

Many will be involved in this effort, from FBI agents to intelligence operatives to the reservists we have called to active duty. All deserve our thanks, and all have our prayers. And tonight, a few miles from the damaged Pentagon, I have a message for our military: Be ready. I've called the Armed Forces to alert, and there is a reason. The hour is coming when America will act, and you will make us proud.

This is not, however, just America's fight. And what is at stake is not just America's freedom. This is the world's fight. This is civilization's fight. This is the fight of all who believe in progress and pluralism, tolerance and freedom.

We ask every nation to join us. We will ask, and we will need, the help of police forces, intelligence services, and banking systems around the world. The United States is grateful that many nations and many international organizations have already responded—with sympathy and with support. Nations from Latin America, to Asia, to Africa, to Europe, to the Islamic world. Perhaps the NATO Charter reflects best the attitude of the world: An attack on one is an attack on all.

The civilized world is rallying to America's side. They understand that if this terror goes unpunished, their own cities, their own citizens may be next. Terror, unanswered, can not only bring down buildings, it can threaten the stability of legitimate governments. And you know what—we're not going to allow it.

Americans should not expect one battle, but a lengthy campaign, unlike any other we have ever seen. It may include dramatic strikes, visible on TV, and covert operations, secret even in success. We will starve terrorists of funding, turn them one against another, drive them from place to place, until there is no refuge or no rest. And we will pursue nations that provide aid or safe haven to terrorism. Every nation, in every region, now has a decision to make. Either you are with us, or you are with the terrorists. From this day forward, any nation that continues to harbor or support terrorism will be regarded by the United States as a hostile regime.

Our nation has been put on notice: We are not immune from attack. We will take defensive measures against terrorism to protect Americans. Today, dozens of federal departments and agencies, as well as state and local governments, have responsibilities affecting homeland security. These efforts must be coordinated at the highest level. So tonight I announce the creation of a Cabinet-level position reporting directly to me—the Office of Homeland Security.

And tonight I also announce a

Americans are asking: What is expected of us? I ask you to live your lives, and hug your children. I know many citizens have fears tonight, and I ask you to be calm and resolute, even in the face of a continuing threat.

I ask you to uphold the values of America, and remember why so many have come here. We are in a fight for our principles, and our first responsibility is to live by them. No one should be singled out for unfair treatment or unkind words because of their ethnic background or religious faith.

I ask you to continue to support the victims of this tragedy with your contributions. Those who want to give can go to a central source of information, libertyunites.org, to find the names of groups providing direct help in New York, Pennsylvania, and Virginia.

The thousands of FBI agents who are now at work in this investigation may need your cooperation, and I ask you to give it. I ask for your patience, with the delays and inconveniences that may accompany tighter security; and for your patience in what will be a long struggle.

I ask your continued participation and confidence in the American economy. Terrorists attacked a symbol of American prosperity. They did not touch its source. America is successful because of the hard work, and creativity, and enterprise of our people. These were the true strengths of our economy before September 11th, and they are our strengths today.

And, finally, please continue praying for the victims of terror and their families, for those in uniform, and for our great country. Prayer has comforted us in sorrow, and will help strengthen us for the journey ahead.

Tonight I thank my fellow Americans for what you have already done and for what you will do. And ladies and gentlemen of the Congress, I thank you, their representatives, for what you have already done and for what we will do together.

Tonight, we face new and sudden national challenges. We will come together to improve air safety, to dramatically expand the number of air marshals on domestic flights, and take new measures to prevent hijacking. We will come together to promote stability and keep our airlines flying, with direct assistance during this emergency.

We will come together to give law enforcement the additional tools it needs to track down terror here at home. We will come together to strengthen our intelligence capabilities to know the plans of terrorists before they act, and find them before they strike.

We will come together to take active steps that strengthen America's economy, and put our people back to work.

Tonight we welcome two leaders who embody the extraordinary spirit of all New Yorkers: Governor George Pataki and Mayor Rudolph Giuliani. As a symbol of America's resolve, my administration will work with Congress, and these two leaders, to show the world that we will rebuild New York City.

After all that has just passed—all the lives taken, and all the possibilities and hopes that died with them—it is natural to wonder if America's future is one of fear. Some speak of an age of terror. I know there are struggles ahead, and dangers to face. But this country will define our times, not be defined by them. As long as the United States of America is determined and strong, this will not be an age of terror; this will be an age of liberty, here and across the world.

Great harm has been done to us. We have suffered great loss. And in our grief and anger we have found our mission and our moment. Freedom and fear are at war. The advance of human freedom—the great achievement of our time, and the great hope of every time—now depends on us. Our nation—this generation—will lift a dark threat of violence from our people and our future. We will rally the world to this cause by our efforts, by our courage. We will not tire, we will not falter, and we will not fail.

It is my hope that in the months and years ahead, life will return almost to normal. We'll go back to our lives and routines, and that is good. Even grief recedes with time and grace. But our resolve must not pass. Each of us will remember what happened that day, and to whom it happened. We'll remember the moment the news came—where we were and what we were doing. Some will remember an image of a fire, or a story of rescue. Some will carry memories of a face and a voice gone forever.

And I will carry this: It is the police shield of a man named George Howard, who died at the World Trade Center trying to save others. It was given to me by his mom, Arlene, as a proud memorial to her son. This is my reminder of lives that ended, and a task that does not end.

I will not forget this wound to our country or those who inflicted it. I will not yield; I will not rest; I will not relent in waging this struggle for freedom and security for the American people.

The course of this conflict is not known, yet its outcome is certain. Freedom and fear, justice and cruelty, have always been at war, and we know that God is not neutral between them.

Fellow citizens, we'll meet violence with patient justice—assured of the rightness of our cause, and confident of the victories to come. In all that lies before us, may God grant us wisdom, and may He watch over the United States of America.

Thank you.

President Bush, with Secretary of State Colin Powell, talks on the steps of the Rose Garden on September 24. Bush signed an executive order that immediately froze U.S. financial assets of and prohibited U.S. transactions with 27 different entities that serve as a front to terrorism.

President Bush is presented a copy of the Holy Koran by Iman Muzammil H. Siddiqi of the Islamic Society of America on September 26 in the Roosevelt Room of the White House, where Bush met with Islamic community leaders. Bush said U.S. efforts to retaliate against Osama bin Laden, the Saudi-born militant he blames for the strikes two weeks ago, require "the best intelligence we can possibly have."

President Bush meets with American Sikh community leaders in the Roosevelt Room of the White House on September 26 to assure the leaders of his support as he plans for a war against terrorism.

On October 2 President Bush announces the reopening of Ronald Reagan Washington National Airport in Alexandria, Virginia, located just across the river from Washington, D.C. Bush said security precautions are expected to include U.S. Marshals on every flight in and out of Reagan National Airport.

President Bush addresses employees of the Central Intelligence Agency (CIA) on September 26 at the agency's headquarters in Washington, D.C. Bush thanked the CIA workers for their long hours and hard work in the wake of the September 11 terrorist attacks.

President Bush and two airline officers look grim shortly after Bush's announcement on September 27 of expanded U.S. aviation security procedures—including more Air Marshals, aircraft cockpit modifications, and new standards for ground security operations—to thousands of airline employees at Chicago's O'Hare International Airport. The slump in air travel since hijackers crashed airliners into the World Trade Center and the Pentagon, has led airlines to announce layoffs in the tens of thousands and deepened the U.S. economic slowdown.

President Bush (center) and New York Governor George Pataki (left) greet firefighters at the Wall Street landing zone on Wednesday, October 3. This is the President's second visit to New York City since the terrorist's bombing and he is expected to meet with National Business Leaders, visit an elementary school, and meet with Fire Engine Company 55.

This photo released by the White House shows President Bush meeting former governor of Pennsylvania Tom Ridge in the Oval Office. Ridge was sworn in as Director of Homeland Security.

PRESIDENT WORKS ON ECONOMIC RECOVERY

THE PRESIDENT: It's an honor to be back in New York City. I want to thank the Mayor and the Governor for welcoming us back. I'm pleased that Secretary Don Evans, and Larry Lindsey from the White House staff, are traveling with me, and I want to thank the business leaders from not only New York, but others who have come from around the country to discuss the state of the nation.

And we've had a very frank discussion about the state of our economy. I think there's no question we all agree that the events of September 11th shocked our economy, just like it shocked the conscience of our nation. But like those terrorists, they can't affect our soul, they can't affect the greatness of America. We all believe that the underpinnings are there for economic recovery.

And we all must do our part. And the federal government has a role to play. Today Secretary Paul O'Neill testified at Congress, saying that the administration believes that we ought to have $60 billion to $75 billion more of stimulus to encourage consumer confidence, to enhance business investment, as well as to take care of displaced workers.

I have shared that with the business leaders here. They understand that there is a role for the federal government, a strong and active role. And I assured them it's a role that we intend to play.

I know there are people hurting in America; there are people who have lost their jobs. But as I assured these leaders, that our government will do everything we can to get our economy growing, to make it as strong as possible. I am saddened by the sight of the World Trade Center, again, once again. But through my tears I do see a much better future for the country.

This is a great nation. It's an entrepreneurial nation; it's a nation that has got such generous and kind people— the leadership, the business leadership here has contributed $150 million to the funds, the variety of funds here in the New York City area, to help people, the victims. It speaks volumes about what America is about.

And I want to thank everybody for coming.

President Bush along with Air Force General Gerry Parski (left) gets a rousing response from military personnel at Travis Air Force Base in California on October 17. Bush is on his way to attend the October 20–21 annual Asia-Pacific Economic Cooperation (APEC) forum in Shanghai, China.

On October 26 President Bush (center) signs into law an antiterrorism bill that expands police and surveillance powers in response to September 11 attacks. With Bush in the East Room of the White House are, from left to right, Rep. Mike Oxley, R-OH, Sen. Orrin Hatch, R-UT, Sen Pat Leahy, D-VT, Sen. Harry Reid, D-NV, and Rep. James Sensenbrenner, R-WI.

President Bush (center) talks with a New York fireman and other personnel on November 11 after attending a memorial service at the site of the World Trade Center to honor the foreign nationals who perished in the terrorist attacks two months ago in New York City.

President Bush speaks at the Georgia World Congress Center in Atlanta on November 9. Bush urged American citizens to help meet the "great national challenge" of eradicating terrorism and cherish the national unity and sense of purpose that emerged from the ashes of September 11 terror strikes.

IMS OF THE WORI
BER 11, 2001

PAN
ORDAN
AZAKHSTAN
ENYA
UNITED NATIONS
UNITED STATES
LEBANON
LIBERIA
LUXEMBOURG
MALAYSIA

MEXICO
NETHERLA
NEW ZEAL
NICARAG
NIGERIA
NORWA
PAKIST
PANAM
PARA
PERU

President Bush and UN Secretary-General Kofi Annan sign a wall of remembrance after a memorial service at the site of the World Trade Center on Sunday, November 11. The service was held in honor of the foreign nationals who perished in the terrorist attacks exactly two months ago.

THE PRESIDENT: Thank you very much. Mr. Speaker, Vice President Cheney, members of Congress, distinguished guests, fellow citizens: As we gather tonight, our nation is at war, our economy is in recession, and the civilized world faces unprecedented dangers. Yet the state of our Union has never been stronger.

We last met in an hour of shock and suffering. In four short months, our nation has comforted the victims, begun to rebuild New York and the Pentagon, rallied a great coalition, captured, arrested, and rid the world of thousands of terrorists, destroyed Afghanistan's terrorist training camps, saved a people from starvation, and freed a country from brutal oppression.

The American flag flies again over our embassy in Kabul. Terrorists who once occupied Afghanistan now occupy cells at Guantanamo Bay. And terrorist leaders who urged followers to sacrifice their lives are running for their own.

America and Afghanistan are now allies against terror. We'll be partners in rebuilding that country. And this evening we welcome the distinguished interim leader of a liberated Afghanistan: Chairman Hamid Karzai.

The last time we met in this chamber, the mothers and daughters of Afghanistan were captives in their own homes, forbidden from working or going to school. Today women are free, and are part of Afghanistan's new government. And we welcome the new Minister of Women's Affairs, Doctor Sima Samar.

Our progress is a tribute to the spirit of the Afghan people, to the resolve of our coalition, and to the might of the United States military. When I called our troops into action, I did so with complete confidence in their courage and skill. And tonight, thanks to them, we are winning the war on terror. The men and women of our Armed Forces have delivered a message now clear to every enemy of the United States: Even 7,000 miles away, across oceans and continents, on mountaintops and in caves—you will not escape the justice of this nation.

For many Americans, these four months have brought sorrow and pain that will never completely go away. Every day a retired firefighter returns to Ground Zero, to feel closer to his two sons who died there. At a memorial in New York, a little boy left his football with a note for his lost father: Dear Daddy, please take this to heaven. I don't want to play football until I can play with you again someday.

Last month, at the grave of her husband, Michael, a CIA officer and Marine who died in Mazur-e Sharif, Shannon Spann said these words of farewell: "Semper Fi, my love." Shannon is with us tonight.

Shannon, I assure you and all who have lost a loved one that our cause is just, and our country will never forget the debt we owe Michael and all who gave their lives for freedom.

Our cause is just, and it continues. Our discoveries in Afghanistan confirmed our worst fears, and showed us the true scope of the task ahead. We have seen the depth of our enemies' hatred in videos, where they laugh about the loss of innocent life. And the depth of their hatred is equaled by the madness of the destruction they design. We have found diagrams of American nuclear power plants and public water facilities, detailed instructions for making chemical weapons, surveillance maps of American cities, and thorough descriptions of landmarks in America and throughout the world.

What we have found in Afghanistan confirms that, far from ending there, our war against terror is only beginning. Most of the 19 men who hijacked planes on September the 11th were trained in Afghanistan's camps, and so were tens of thousands of others. Thousands of dangerous killers, schooled in the methods of murder, often supported by outlaw regimes, are now spread throughout the world like ticking time bombs, set to go off without warning.

Thanks to the work of our law enforcement officials and coalition partners, hundreds of terrorists have been arrested. Yet, tens of thousands of trained terrorists are still at large. These enemies view the entire world as a battlefield, and we must pursue them wherever they are. So long as training camps operate, so long as nations harbor terrorists, freedom is at risk. And America and our allies must not, and will not, allow it.

Our nation will continue to be steadfast and patient and persistent in the pursuit of two great objectives. First, we will shut down terrorist camps, disrupt terrorist plans, and bring terrorists to justice. And, second, we must prevent the terrorists and regimes who seek chemical, biological, or nuclear weapons from threatening the United States and the world.

Our military has put the terror training camps of Afghanistan out of business, yet camps still exist in at least a dozen countries. A terrorist underworld— including groups like Hamas, Hezbollah, Islamic Jihad, Jaish-i-Mohammed— operates in remote jungles and deserts, and hides in the centers of large cities.

While the most visible military action is in Afghanistan, America is acting elsewhere. We now have troops in the Philippines, helping to train that country's armed forces to go after terrorist cells that have executed an American, and still hold hostages. Our soldiers, working with the Bosnian government, seized terrorists who were plotting to bomb our embassy. Our Navy is patrolling the coast of Africa to block the shipment of weapons and the establishment of terrorist camps in Somalia.

My hope is that all nations will heed our call, and eliminate the terrorist parasites who threaten their countries and our own. Many nations are acting forcefully. Pakistan is now cracking down on terror, and I admire the strong leadership of President Musharraf.

But some governments will be timid in the face of terror. And make no mistake about it: If they do not act, America will.

Our second goal is to prevent regimes that sponsor terror from threatening America or our friends and allies with weapons of mass destruction. Some of these regimes have been pretty quiet since September the 11th. But we know their true nature. North Korea is a regime arming with missiles and weapons of mass destruction, while starving its citizens.

Iran aggressively pursues these weapons and exports terror, while an unelected few repress the Iranian people's hope for freedom.

Iraq continues to flaunt its hostility toward America and to support terror. The Iraqi regime has plotted to develop anthrax, and nerve gas, and nuclear weapons for over a decade. This is a regime that has already used poison gas to murder thousands of its own citizens—leaving the bodies of mothers huddled over their dead children. This is a regime that agreed to international inspections—then kicked out the inspectors. This is a regime that has something to hide from the civilized world.

States like these, and their terrorist allies, constitute an axis of evil, arming to threaten the peace of the world. By seeking weapons of mass destruction, these regimes pose a grave and growing danger. They could provide these arms to terrorists, giving them the means to match their hatred. They could attack our allies or attempt to blackmail the United States. In any of these cases, the price of indifference would be catastrophic.

We will work closely with our coalition to deny terrorists and their state sponsors the materials, technology, and expertise to make and deliver weapons of mass destruction. We will develop and deploy effective missile defenses to protect America and our allies from sudden attack. And all nations should know: America will do what is necessary to ensure our nation's security.

We'll be deliberate, yet time is not on our side. I will not wait on events, while dangers gather. I will not stand by, as peril draws closer and closer. The United States of America will not permit the world's most dangerous regimes to threaten us with the world's most destructive weapons.

Our war on terror is well begun, but it is only begun. This campaign may not be finished on our watch—yet it must be and it will be waged on our watch.

We can't stop short. If we stop now—leaving terror camps intact and terror states unchecked—our sense of security would be false and temporary. History has called America and our allies to action, and it is both our responsibility and our privilege to fight freedom's fight.

Our first priority must always be the security of our nation, and that will be reflected in the budget I send to Congress. My budget supports three great goals for America: We will win this war; we'll protect our homeland; and we will revive our economy.

September the 11th brought out the best in America, and the best in this Congress. And I join the American people in applauding your unity and resolve. Now Americans deserve to have this same spirit directed toward addressing problems here at home. I'm a proud member of my party—yet as we act to win the war, protect our people, and create jobs in America, we must act, first and foremost, not as Republicans, not as Democrats, but as Americans.

It costs a lot to fight this war. We have spent more than a billion dollars a month—over $30 million a day—and we must be prepared for future operations. Afghanistan proved that expensive precision weapons defeat the enemy and spare innocent lives, and we need more of them. We need to replace aging aircraft and make our military more agile, to put our troops anywhere in the world quickly and safely. Our men and women in uniform deserve the best weapons, the best equipment, the best training—and they also deserve another pay raise.

My budget includes the largest increase in defense spending in two decades—because while the price of freedom and security is high, it is never too high. Whatever it costs to defend our country, we will pay.

The next priority of my budget is to do everything possible to protect our citizens and strengthen our nation against the ongoing threat of another attack. Time and distance from the events of September the 11th will not make us safer unless we act on its lessons. America is no longer protected by vast oceans. We are protected from attack only by vigorous action abroad, and increased vigilance at home.

My budget nearly doubles funding for a sustained strategy of homeland security, focused on four key areas: bioterrorism, emergency response, airport and border security, and improved intelligence. We will develop vaccines to fight anthrax and other deadly diseases. We'll increase funding to help states and communities train and equip our heroic police and firefighters. We will improve intelligence collection and sharing, expand patrols at our borders, strengthen the security of air travel, and use technology to track the arrivals and departures of visitors to the United States.

Homeland security will make America not only stronger, but, in many ways, better. Knowledge gained from bioterrorism research will improve public health. Stronger police and fire departments will mean safer neighborhoods. Stricter border enforcement will help combat illegal drugs. And as government works to better secure our homeland, America will continue to depend on the eyes and ears of alert citizens.

A few days before Christmas, an airline flight attendant spotted a passenger lighting a match. The crew and passengers quickly subdued the man, who had been trained by al Qaeda and was armed with explosives. The people on that plane were alert and, as a result, likely saved nearly 200 lives. And tonight we welcome and thank flight attendants Hermis Moutardier and Christina Jones.

Once we have funded our national security and our homeland security, the final great priority of my budget is economic security for the American people. To achieve these great national objectives—to win the war, protect the homeland, and revitalize our economy—our budget will run a deficit that will be small and short-term, so long as Congress restrains spending and acts in a fiscally responsible manner. We have clear priorities and we must act at home with the same purpose and resolve we have shown overseas: We'll prevail in the war, and we will defeat this recession.

Americans who have lost their jobs need our help and I support extending unemployment benefits and direct assistance for health care coverage. Yet, American workers want more than unemployment checks—they want a steady paycheck. When America works, America prospers, so my economic security plan can be summed up in one word: jobs.

Good jobs begin with good schools, and here we've made a fine start. Republicans and Democrats worked together to achieve historic education reform so that no child is left behind. I was proud to work with members of both parties: Chairman John Boehner and Congressman George Miller. Senator Judd Gregg. And I was so proud of our work, I even had nice things to say about my friend Ted Kennedy. I know the folks at the Crawford coffee shop couldn't believe I'd say such a thing, but our work on this bill shows what is possible if we set aside posturing and focus on results.

There is more to do. We need to prepare our children to read and succeed in school with improved Head Start and early childhood development programs.

We must upgrade our teacher colleges and teacher training and launch a major recruiting drive with a great goal for America: a quality teacher in every classroom.

Good jobs also depend on reliable and affordable energy. This Congress must act to encourage conservation, promote technology, build infrastructure, and it must act to increase energy production at home so America is less dependent on foreign oil.

Good jobs depend on expanded trade. Selling into new markets creates new jobs, so I ask Congress to finally approve trade promotion authority. On these two key issues, trade and energy, the House of Representatives has acted to create jobs, and I urge the Senate to pass this legislation.

Good jobs depend on sound tax policy. Last year, some in this hall thought my tax relief plan was too small; some thought it was too big. But when the checks arrived in the mail, most Americans thought tax relief was just about right. Congress listened to the people and responded by reducing tax rates, doubling the child credit, and ending the death tax. For the sake of long-term growth and to help Americans plan for the future, let's make these tax cuts permanent.

The way out of this recession, the way to create jobs, is to grow the economy by encouraging investment in factories and equipment, and by speeding up tax relief so people have more money to spend. For the sake of American workers, let's pass a stimulus package.

Good jobs must be the aim of welfare reform. As we reauthorize these important reforms, we must always remember the goal is to reduce dependency on government and offer every American the dignity of a job.

Americans know economic security can vanish in an instant without health security. I ask Congress to join me this year to enact a patients' bill of rights, to give uninsured workers credits to help buy health coverage, to approve an historic increase in the spending for veterans' health, and to give seniors a sound and modern Medicare system that includes coverage for prescription drugs.

A good job should lead to security in retirement. I ask Congress to enact new safeguards for 401K and pension plans.

Employees who have worked hard and saved all their lives should not have to risk losing everything if their company fails. Through stricter accounting standards and tougher disclosure requirements, corporate America must be made more accountable to employees and shareholders and held to the highest standards of conduct.

Retirement security also depends upon keeping the commitments of Social Security, and we will. We must make Social Security financially stable and allow personal retirement accounts for younger workers who choose them.

Members, you and I will work together in the months ahead on other issues: productive farm policy, cleaner environment, broader home ownership, especially among minorities, and ways to encourage the good work of charities and faith-based groups. I ask you to join me on these important domestic issues in the same spirit of cooperation we've applied to our war against terrorism.

During these last few months, I've been humbled and privileged to see the true character of this country in a time of testing. Our enemies believed America was weak and materialistic, that we would splinter in fear and selfishness. They were as wrong as they are evil.

The American people have responded magnificently, with courage and compassion, strength and resolve. As I have met the heroes, hugged the families, and looked into the tired faces of rescuers, I have stood in awe of the American people.

And I hope you will join me—I hope you will join me in expressing thanks to one American for the strength and calm and comfort she brings to our nation in crisis, our First Lady, Laura Bush.

None of us would ever wish the evil that was done on September the 11th. Yet after America was attacked, it was as if our entire country looked into a mirror and saw our better selves. We were reminded that we are citizens, with obligations to each other, to our country, and to history. We began to think less of the goods we can accumulate, and more about the good we can do.

For too long our culture has said, "If it feels good, do it." Now America is embracing a new ethic and a new creed: "Let's roll." In the sacrifice of soldiers,

the fierce brotherhood of firefighters, and the bravery and generosity of ordinary citizens, we have glimpsed what a new culture of responsibility could look like. We want to be a nation that serves goals larger than self. We've been offered a unique opportunity, and we must not let this moment pass.

My call tonight is for every American to commit at least two years—4,000 hours over the rest of your lifetime—to the service of your neighbors and your nation. Many are already serving, and I thank you. If you aren't sure how to help, I've got a good place to start. To sustain and extend the best that has emerged in America, I invite you to join the new USA Freedom Corps. The Freedom Corps will focus on three areas of need: responding in case of crisis at home; rebuilding our communities; and extending American compassion throughout the world.

One purpose of the USA Freedom Corps will be homeland security. America needs retired doctors and nurses who can be mobilized in major emergencies; volunteers to help police and fire departments; transportation and utility workers well-trained in spotting danger.

Our country also needs citizens working to rebuild our communities. We need mentors to love children, especially children whose parents are in prison. And we need more talented teachers in troubled schools. USA Freedom Corps will expand and improve the good efforts of AmeriCorps and Senior Corps to recruit more than 200,000 new volunteers.

And America needs citizens to extend the compassion of our country to every part of the world. So we will renew the promise of the Peace Corps, double its volunteers over the next five years, and ask it to join a new effort to encourage development and education and opportunity in the Islamic world.

This time of adversity offers a unique moment of opportunity—a moment we must seize to change our culture. Through the gathering momentum of millions of acts of service and decency and kindness, I know we can overcome evil with greater good. And we have a great opportunity during this time of war to lead the world toward the values that will bring lasting peace.

All fathers and mothers, in all societies, want their children to be educated, and

live free from poverty and violence. No people on earth yearn to be oppressed, or aspire to servitude, or eagerly await the midnight knock of the secret police.

If anyone doubts this, let them look to Afghanistan, where the Islamic "street" greeted the fall of tyranny with song and celebration. Let the skeptics look to Islam's own rich history, with its centuries of learning, and tolerance and progress. America will lead by defending liberty and justice because they are right and true and unchanging for all people everywhere.

No nation owns these aspirations, and no nation is exempt from them. We have no intention of imposing our culture. But America will always stand firm for the non-negotiable demands of human dignity: the rule of law; limits on the power of the state; respect for women; private property; free speech; equal justice; and religious tolerance.

America will take the side of brave men and women who advocate these values around the world, including the Islamic world, because we have a greater objective than eliminating threats and containing resentment. We seek a just and peaceful world beyond the war on terror.

In this moment of opportunity, a common danger is erasing old rivalries. America is working with Russia and China and India, in ways we have never

before, to achieve peace and prosperity. In every region, free markets and free trade and free societies are proving their power to lift lives. Together with friends and allies from Europe to Asia, and Africa to Latin America, we will demonstrate that the forces of terror cannot stop the momentum of freedom.

The last time I spoke here, I expressed the hope that life would return to normal. In some ways, it has. In others, it never will. Those of us who have lived through these challenging times have been changed by them. We've come to know truths that we will never question: Evil is real, and it must be opposed. Beyond all differences of race or creed, we are one country, mourning together and facing danger together. Deep in the American character, there is honor, and it is stronger than cynicism. And many have discovered again that even in tragedy—especially in tragedy—God is near.

In a single instant, we realized that this will be a decisive decade in the history of liberty, that we've been called to a unique role in human events. Rarely has the world faced a choice more clear or consequential.

Our enemies send other people's children on missions of suicide and murder. They embrace tyranny and death as a cause and a creed. We stand for a different

Mrs. Lynne Cheney (left); Mrs. Shannon Spann (second from left), widow of a CIA operative killed in Afghanistan; and First Lady Laura Bush (right) applaud Afghanistan Interim Authority Chairman Hamid Karzai (center), during President Bush's State of the Union address on January 29 on Capitol Hill in Washington, D.C. Bush said "our nation is at war, our economy is in recession, and the civilized world faces unprecedented dangers."

choice, made long ago, on the day of our founding. We affirm it again today. We choose freedom and the dignity of every life.

Steadfast in our purpose, we now press on. We have known freedom's price. We have shown freedom's power. And in this great conflict, my fellow Americans, we will see freedom's victory.

Thank you all. May God bless.

The Prime Minister

British Prime Minister Tony Blair arrives at 10 Downing Street, London, following the news that the World Trade Center in New York and the Pentagon in Washington were both hit by aircraft in what looks to be a terrorist attack.

PRIME MINISTER TONY BLAIR HAS MADE THE FOLLOWING STATEMENT IN RESPONSE TO THE TERRORIST ATTACKS IN THE UNITED STATES:

During a press conference in London on September 12, Mr. Blair said that Parliament will be recalled in the wake of the terrorist attacks in the U.S.

The full horror of what has happened in the United States earlier today is now becoming clearer. It is hard even to contemplate the utter carnage and terror which has engulfed so many innocent people. We've offered President Bush and the American people our solidarity, our profound sympathy, and our prayers. But it is plain that citizens of many countries around the world, including Britain, will have been caught up in this terror. As for those that carried out these attacks, there are no adequate words of condemnation. Their barbarism will stand as their shame for all eternity.

As I said earlier, this mass terrorism is the new evil in our world. The people who perpetrate it have no regard whatsoever for the sanctity or value of human life, and we, the democracies of the world, must come together to defeat it and eradicate it. This is not a battle between the United States of America and terrorism, but between the free and democratic world and terrorism. We, therefore, here in Britain stand shoulder to shoulder with our American friends in this hour of tragedy, and we, like them, will not rest until this evil is driven from our world.

Prime Minister Tony Blair reads to the gathered relatives during a special service at the St. Thomas Church in New York on September 20, held for the British victims of the terrorist attack on the World Trade Center.

112

PRIME MINISTER BLAIR PLEDGES SOLIDARITY

THE PRESIDENT: It's my honor to welcome my friend, and friend to America, Prime Minister Tony Blair to the White House. I appreciate him coming to America in our time of need. One of the first phone calls I got after that terrible day was from the Prime Minister. He was reassuring to me. He was—he showed to be a true friend, and I appreciate that.

I'm so honored you're here. And I look forward to giving a speech tonight. The Prime Minister has kindly agreed to come and listen to it. So I'm not going to answer any questions tonight. I'm going to let my speech be exactly what I want to say.

In the meantime, the Prime Minister has agreed to say a few comments, and then take a couple of questions from you.

PRIME MINISTER BLAIR: Thank you, Mr. President. It's my honor to be here, and also to pay tribute to your leadership at this immensely difficult time. I was in New York earlier today, and it's perhaps only when you are actually there that the full enormity and horror of what happened comes home to you.

And I said then, I would like to repeat, that my father's generation went through the experience of the Second World War, when Britain was under attack, during the days of the Blitz. And there was one nation and one people that, above all, stood side by side with us at that time. And that nation was America, and those people were the American people. And I say to you, we stand side by side with you now, without hesitation.

This is a struggle that concerns us all, the whole of the democratic and civilized and free world. And we have to do two things very clearly; we have to bring to account those responsible, and then we have to set about at every single level, in every way that we can, dismantling the apparatus of terror, and eradicating the evil of mass terrorism in our world.

And I know that America, Britain, and all our allies will stand united together in that task. And I give you, on behalf of our country, our solidarity, our sympathy, and our support.

British Prime Minister Tony Blair (left) and Mayor Giuliani (right) applaud with First Lady Laura Bush on September 20, as President Bush addresses a joint session of the U.S. Congress on Capitol Hill in Washington, D.C. Bush called the joint session to explain his position on the U.S. reaction to the terrorist strikes on the World Trade Center and the Pentagon.

On September 27, Prime Minister Blair met with community leaders to reassure them that whatever action occurs in Afghanistan is against terrorist networks and not Muslim people and Islam.

Prime Minister Blair addresses an emergency session of the House of Commons in London on October 4, to tell MPs, recalled from the summer recess for the second time, about the latest development in the antiterror coalition. He is expected to meet Russia's President Putin in Moscow later in the day at the start of a round of diplomacy amid speculation that military action against terror bases in Afghanistan would be launched within days.

Prime Minister Blair (left) and Pakistan President Pervez Musharraf (right) in a press conference at the executive house in Islamabad on October 5. Britain and Pakistan agreed that any post-Taliban government in Afghanistan must be broad-based and include all key ethnic groups, including the dominant Pashtun community.

Prime Minister Tony Blair stands alongside Indian Prime Minister Atal Bihari Vajpayee before a press conference at the Prime Minister's residence in Delhi on October 6.

PRIME MINISTER TONY BLAIR:
As you will know from the announcement by President Bush military action against targets inside Afghanistan has begun.

I can confirm that U.K. forces are engaged in this action. I want to pay tribute, if I might, right at the outset to Britain's armed forces. There is no greater strength for a British Prime Minister and the British nation at a time like this than to know that the forces we are calling upon are amongst the very best in the world.

They and their families are, of course, carrying an immense burden at this moment and will be feeling deep anxiety, as will the British people. But we can take pride in their courage, their sense of duty and the esteem with which they're held throughout the world.

No country lightly commits forces to military action and the inevitable risks

involved but we made it clear following the attacks upon the United States on September 11th that we would take part in action once it was clear who was responsible.

There is no doubt in my mind, nor in the mind of anyone who has been through all the available evidence, including intelligence material, that these attacks were carried out by the al Qaeda network masterminded by Osama bin Laden. Equally it is clear that his network is harbored and supported by the Taliban regime inside Afghanistan.

It is now almost a month since the atrocity occurred, it is more than two weeks since an ultimatum was delivered to the Taliban to yield up the terrorists or face the consequences. It is clear beyond doubt that they will not do this. They were given the choice of siding with justice or siding

with terror and they chose to side with terror.

There are three parts all equally important to the operation of which we're engaged: military, diplomatic, and humanitarian. The military action we are taking will be targeted against places we know to be involved in the operation of terror or against the military apparatus of the Taliban. This military plan has been put together mindful of our determination to do all we humanly can to avoid civilian casualties.

I cannot disclose, obviously, how long this action will last but we will act with reason and resolve. We have set the objectives to eradicate Osama bin Laden's network of terror and to take action against the Taliban regime that is sponsoring it. As to the precise British involvement, I can confirm that last Wednesday the U.S.

government made a specific request that a number of U.K. military assets be used in the operation that has now begun. And I gave authority for these assets to be deployed. They include the base at Diego Garcia, reconnaissance and flight support aircraft, and missile firing submarines. Missile firing submarines are in use tonight. The air assets will be available for use in the coming days.

The United States are providing the bulk of the force required in leading this operation. But this is an international effort as well. The U.K., France, Germany, Australia, and Canada have also committed themselves to the operation.

On the diplomatic and political front in the time I've been Prime Minister, I cannot recall a situation that has commanded so quickly such a powerful coalition of support and not just from those countries directly involved in military action but from many others in all parts of the world. The coalition has, I believe, strengthened, not weakened, in the twenty-six days since the atrocity occurred. And this is in no small measure due to the statesmanship of President Bush to whom I pay tribute tonight.

The world understands that whilst, of course, there are dangers in acting the dangers of inaction are far, far greater. The threat of further such outrages, the threat to our economies, the threat to the stability of the world.

On the humanitarian front we are assembling a coalition of support for refugees in and outside Afghanistan, which is as vital as the military coalition.

Even before September 11, four million Afghans were on the move. There are two million refugees in Pakistan and one and a half million in Iran. We have to act for humanitarian reasons to alleviate the appalling suffering of the Afghan people and deliver stability so that people from that region stay in that region. Britain, of course, is heavily involved in actually [indistinct] effort.

So we are taking action therefore on all those three fronts: military, diplomatic, and humanitarian. I also want to say very directly to the British people why this matters so much directly to Britain. First let us not forget that the attacks of September 11 represented the worst terrorist outrage against British citizens in our history. The murder of British citizens, whether it happens overseas or not, is an attack upon Britain. But even if no British citizen had died, it would be right to act.

This atrocity was an attack on us all, on people of all faiths, and people of none. We know the al Qaeda network threatens Europe, including Britain, and, indeed, any nation throughout the world that does not share their fanatical views. So we have a direct interest in acting in our own self-defense to protect British lives. It was also an attack (indistinct) just on lives but on livelihoods. We can see since the 11th of September how economic confidence has suffered with all that means for British jobs and British industry. Our prosperity and standard of living, therefore, require us to deal with this terrorist threat.

We act also because the al Qaeda network

and the Taliban regime are funded in large part on the drugs trade. Ninety percent of all the heroin sold on British streets originates from Afghanistan. Stopping that trade is, again, directly in our interests.

I wish to say finally, as I've said many times before, that this is not a war with Islam. It angers me, as it angers the vast majority of Muslims, to hear bin Laden and his associates described as Islamic terrorists. They are terrorists pure and simple. Islam is a peaceful and tolerant religion and the acts of these people are wholly contrary to the teachings of the Koran.

These are difficult and testing times therefore for all of us. People are bound to be concerned about what the terrorists may seek to do in response. I should say there is at present no specific credible threat to the U.K. that we know of and that we have in place tried and tested contingency plans, which are the best possible response to any further attempts at terror.

This, of course, is a moment of the utmost gravity for the world. None of the leaders involved in this action want war. None of our nations want it. We are a peaceful people. But we know that sometimes to safeguard peace we have to fight. Britain has learned that lesson many times in our history. We only do it if the cause is just but this cause is just. The murder of almost seven thousand innocent people in America was an attack on our freedom, our way of life, an attack on civilized values the world over. We waited so that those responsible could be yielded up by those shielding them. That offer was refused, we have now no choice so we will act. And our determination in acting is total. We will not let up or rest until our objectives are met in full. Thank you.

Prime Minister Tony Blair in Downing Street with Foreign Secretary Jack Straw (left), Deputy Prime Minister John Prescott (center left), and Defense Secretary Geoff Hoon (right) making a statement as the war against terrorism started with British forces playing a part in the air assault on the Afghan capital of Kabul and other cities.

Prime Minister Blair (center) chairs a special Cabinet meeting in Downing Street. He traveled to the House of Commons to tell MPs about the latest development in the military action against terror. Members of the Conservative Party returned for the prime minister's statement and subsequent debate from their conference in Blackpool on October 8.

Prime Minister Blair, addressing the House of Commons, London, in a special meeting called in response to the British and American attacks on Afghanistan on October 8.

Prime Minister Blair (center) talks with leaders of all of Britain's main religions who gathered to discuss military and humanitarian operations in Afghanistan on October 8.

Prime Minister Blair with the leader of the United Arab Emirates, Sheikh Zayed Al Nayan, in Geneva on October 9. The sheikh has now backed the international coalition despite his country having previously been one of only three nations officially to recognize Afghanistan's Taliban regime.

Prime Minister Blair is interviewed in London on October 9. He promised the international coalition would not walk away from Afghanistan after the immediate conflict with Osama bin Laden and the Taliban regime was over.

Prime Minister Blair addresses the troops at Al Sha'afa camp in north Oman as part of a two-day diplomatic visit to the area. Al Sha'afa base is the center of Operation Swift Sword II, involving more than 20,000 British servicemen and women in the biggest deployment since the Gulf War, although the forces are not involved in the current attacks on Afghanistan.

PRIME MINISTER: "We will not stop until our mission is complete."

In a speech to the Welsh Assembly on the war against terror, Prime Minister Tony Blair said: "It is important we never forget why we are doing it. Important we never forget how we felt watching the planes fly into the Twin Towers. Never forget those answering machine messages. Never forget how we felt imagining how mothers told children they were about to die."

During the speech, the Prime Minister urged people not to forget the reasons for the military campaign in Afghanistan, saying: "If we do not act against al Qaeda and the Taliban, al Qaeda will have perpetrated this atrocity, the Taliban will have sheltered them, and we will have done nothing. We will have done nothing despite the fact, also inescapable, that they intend to commit more atrocities unless we yield to their demands, which include the eradication of Israel, the killing of all Jews and the setting up of fundamentalist states in all parts of the Arab and Muslim world."

The Prime Minister reiterated the aims and objectives of the coalition, saying: "Our objectives are clear: to close down the al Qaeda network, bring bin Laden and his associates to justice and because the Taliban regime have chosen to side with al Qaeda, to remove them."

"The means we use will be air power; ground operations, as and when in furtherance of our aims; support to the Northern Alliance and other anti-Taliban regime elements; and building up a strong political and diplomatic coalition against the present Taliban regime inside and outside necessary Afghanistan."

Outlining the progress made by the coalition, Mr. Blair said: "We have destroyed the Taliban air force, put Taliban airfields and air defense systems out of action; destroyed all the main al Qaeda camps; profoundly damaged Taliban command and control facilities, and dramatically reduced their capacity to communicate with their forces in the field."

During his speech, the Prime Minister stressed that the war in Afghanistan is not a conventional conflict, he continued: "It is a battle to allow Afghans themselves to retake control of their country and in doing so, to close down the threat posed by the present rules. The political and diplomatic go hand in hand with the military. And we simply cannot and should not disclose the exact nature of the ground operations we intend to undertake."

Concluding his speech, Mr. Blair paid tribute to the support shown by Muslim leaders: "Now is a time for people of all races and all faiths in Britain to stand together. That is exactly what Muslim leaders in Wales and across Britain have done with their forthright condemnation of the atrocities of September 11, and I thank them for it."

Prime Minister Blair visiting British troops in Oman on October 10. Mr. Blair joined troops in a makeshift mess hall for a lunch of curry, rice, and peas. He made a tour of the Al Sha'afa base, the command center of Operation Swift Sword II, involving more than 20,000 British servicemen and women in the biggest deployment since the Gulf War.

Prime Minister Blair, on a flight to Cairo on the latest leg of his Middle East diplomatic mission after the heaviest wave yet of air strikes against Afghanistan. During his visit, Mr. Blair will have talks with President Hosni Mubarak, both on the international fight against terrorism and the need to put the Middle East peace process back on track.

Prime Minister Blair takes questions from the Arabic media on events in Afghanistan on October 18. He warned that the coming weeks would be the "most testing time in the current campaign against international terrorism."

The Mayor

New York City Mayor Rudolph Giuliani (right) consoles Anita Deblase (left), of New York, whose son, James Deblase, 44, is missing, at the site of the World Trade Center. "He's at the bottom of the rubble," she said. James Deblase worked for Cantor Fitzgerald at the World Trade Center.

"The best way to deal with this is not only to deal with our own grief," the mayor told reporters, "but also show we're not cowered by it, that we're not afraid and go about our business."

But going about business remains difficult, particularly in lower Manhattan where a dull brown haze of debris and smoke continues to hover at suffocating levels. As workers remain focused on retrieving victims, the task of getting the city back in full working order following Tuesday's terrorist attacks remains almost too daunting for experts to assess.

Christopher Silver, a professor of urban and regional planning at the University of Illinois in Chicago, points out that the compact infrastructure and high rise architecture of New York City made it "much more vulnerable to catastrophe" and so recovery is made much more difficult.

The mayor estimated the task of removing debris alone will likely take at least two to three weeks. He said workers drove 120 full dump trunks out of the city last night and have begun to chip away at the heaps of tangled debris that have blocked access to the site by rescue vehicles. That work will continue using trucks as well as barges.

Efforts to remove debris and recover victims has been made more difficult by the haunting realization that hundreds of fellow rescue workers who responded to the scene Tuesday were killed.

Other issues that city officials are now grappling with are how to ensure food and water supplies continue to enter affected areas of the city, reopening schools that remained closed citywide today, and restoring power to southern Manhattan. Electric service was suspended Tuesday on the western swath of lower Manhattan south of Chambers street.

The mayor said most schools will reopen Thursday, two hours later than normally scheduled times. However, schools on the Lower East Side of Manhattan still don't have power and those below 14th Street will remain closed. Generators have been brought in to use in the school buildings. Con Edison, the city's main power company, has also moved a large group of generators to Randall's Island to the east of Manhattan to bolster power supplies. The electrical supply company has been unavailable for comment but released a statement Tuesday saying its crews "are continuing to work closely with all emergency personnel."

Phone companies also worked to get call-handling capacity back to normal after equipment damage and nearly double normal demand immediately following the attack sometimes made it difficult to get calls through.

"The area around lower Manhattan, particularly around the World Trade Center, has more telecommunications traffic and equipment than anywhere else in the world, and right now we just don't know how significantly the network has been affected," said John H. Johnson, a Verizon Wireless spokesman. "There are a number of facilities underground that sustained the equivalent of several earthquakes yesterday."

Verizon was especially affected, with a land-line switching station and 10 cellular sites routed through the World Trade Center damaged. Technicians gained access to the 200,000-line switching station today and still were assessing damage. However, Verizon said cell-phone capacity was nearly restored thanks to the temporary installation of mobile equipment and refocusing toward lower Manhattan of equipment in nearby areas such as New Jersey.

A Sprint spokesman said that the company also was working to compensate for damaged cell sites near the Trade Center by redirecting nearby equipment. Other Sprint services elsewhere in the city also were intermittently affected by spot power outages.

At the same time, Verizon and other wireless companies said they donated thousands of cell phones, other equipment and services to emergency personnel— and phone company efforts during the crisis yielded a statement of praise from Michael K. Powell, chairman of the Federal Communications Commission.

"I am grateful for the tireless and heroic efforts of those in the telecommunications industry who are working hard to keep our most fundamental communications systems—such as telephone service, wireless phone and television service— operating efficiently under the circumstances," said Powell's statement. "This is a difficult time for everyone and we must be patient."

Mayor Giuliani (right) gives a tour of ground zero to U.N. Secretary-General Kofi Annan (center) and New York Governor George Pataki (left) on September 18.

President Bush surveys the damage at the site of the World Trade Center with Mayor Giuliani and a New York City Fire Department official on September 14.

Mayor Giuliani hangs his head on September 18 after stating that he does not have much hope for finding survivors in the rubble of ground zero. Recovery efforts continue for victims of last week's attack.

Mayor Giuliani leads a group in flag waving (1st row, left to right) Mayor Giuliani, New York Gov. George Pataki, Acting New Jersey Gov. Donald T. DiFrancesco, (2nd row, left to right) New York Fire Department Rabbi Joseph Potasnik, Sen. Charles Schumer, Sen. Hillary Clinton, former President Bill Clinton, and former New York City Mayor Ed Koch (behind Clinton) at the "A Prayer for America" memorial service at New York's Yankee Stadium on September 23 to remember the victims of the World Trade Center attack.

Mayor Rudolph Giuliani addresses the United Nations on Monday, October 1, at the UN headquarters in New York. Giuliani spoke to the UN members prior to their meeting on international terrorism.

Mayor Giuliani (center) points out areas of devastation to members of Congress on October 1. More than 100 congressional members toured the site of the World Trade Center.

Britain's Prince Andrew (center) shakes hands with a World Trade Center ironworker (right) at the opening of the ice-skating rink at Rockefeller Center in New York. Former Olympic champion JoJo Starbuck (2nd left) and Mayor Giuliani (left) look on.

New York City Mayor Rudolph Giuliani is seen at the World Trade Center disaster site after a short interfaith memorial service at the disaster area on October 11. One month after two hijacked airliners toppled the World Trade Center, hundreds at the site stopped for a moment of silence at 8:48 A.M. to remember the missing and the dead.

President Bush (right) and Mayor Giuliani (left) listen to Muslim Cleric Iman Ahmed Dewider deliver a prayer in the memorial service at the site of the World Trade Center to honor the foreign nationals who perished in the terrorist attacks two months earlier.

Secretary of Defense Donald Rumsfeld (left) tours ground zero with Mayor Giuliani (right) on November 14.

Mayor Giuliani (left) speaks to former South African President Nelson Mandela on November 15 about the collapse of the World Trade Center towers.

Israeli Prime Minister Ariel Sharon (right) and Mayor Giuliani (left) embrace after visiting ground zero on November 30.

Spanish President Jose Maria Aznar (left) and Mayor Giuliani (right) visit ground zero on November 30. At center is Spanish first lady Ana Botella.

Mayor Giuliani (center) serves green beans to a National Guardsman during a Christmas dinner served by the Salvation Army for workers at ground zero.

Mayor Giuliani speaking at St. Paul's Chapel, December

Thank you very, very much.

People ask where I get my energy. Well, it's really simple. It comes from you. It comes from here. What I mean by that is that my strength and energy comes entirely from the people of the City of New York. And it comes from a place like this, St. Paul's Chapel. This is a House of God, and it's one of the homes of our Republic.

Although I have to leave you as the mayor soon, I resume the much more honorable title of citizen: citizen of New York and citizen of the United States. The reason I chose to give my farewell address here is because this chapel is thrice-hallowed ground. This is a place of really special importance to people who have a feeling and a sense and an emotion and an understanding of patriotism. It is hallowed by the fact that it was consecrated as a house of God in 1766. That's a long time ago. And then in April of 1789, George Washington came here after he was inaugurated as the first President of our Republic. He prayed right here in this church, which makes it very sacred ground to people who care deeply about America. Then it was consecrated one more time, on September 11th.

When I walked in here from City Hall, I looked up, because every time I've walked toward this church I saw the Twin Towers. This church existed for many years in the shadow of the Twin Towers. On September 11, when the Twin Towers were viciously attacked and came crashing to the ground, they destroyed buildings all around, and did damage as far as City Hall and the southern part of Battery Park City. They covered this whole area with debris and body parts, and in many ways damaged buildings. This chapel remained, not only not destroyed, but not a single window was broken. And I think there's some very special significance in that.

I remember after the attack on the World Trade Center, it just came very naturally for me to say to people, "Do not engage in group blame. Do not go single out people who are Arab-Americans and blame the attack on the World Trade Center on them." Because the people who attacked the World Trade Center, we weren't even sure exactly who it was then, but the people who attacked the World Trade Center obviously are vicious criminals of the worst kind, and there isn't a single group that sits out there that doesn't have among them vicious criminals of some kind. Every ethnic group, religious group, racial group, has some bad, really bad people in that group. And then the question becomes, are you the kind of prejudiced, irrational human being that defines the group based on the bad people in that group—which means you're going to end up hating everybody—or do you kind of get beyond that, and see that in fact, with every group, most people are decent people who are trying to do the same thing that you're doing? I think New York allows more and more people to see that than any place else, because we keep bumping into each other all the time. People who look different than you do, and they have different outfits, and they talk different languages, and they wear different clothes and they say different things. And if you're a person of some degree of common sense and intelligence, that experience opens you up to the feeling that people are basically all the same. And it's the greatest strength we have.

The greatest strength that we have as a city is immigration and keeping ourselves open to people. And we shouldn't allow what has happened to us in the last three months to stop that in any way at all. We should continue to be open to people. That doesn't mean we shouldn't have more security. That doesn't mean we should be open to people with criminal backgrounds. It doesn't mean that we shouldn't in a very proper and appropriate and even tough way screen the people who come here to make sure that we're not letting terrorists in. But it does mean that we should continue to be a city and a country that's open to new people coming here from all over the world…You know, our enemies insanely committed suicide to serve some irrational purpose. And they think that we're afraid to die. They used to think that we're afraid to die for what we believe in. And the reality is that we don't want to die, and we don't believe that it's our right to make that choice for ourselves. We think God only has that right. But the reality is that we're just two blocks from the site in which hundreds and hundreds of men and women freely, by choice, gave up their life. First to protect the lives of other people and secondly to preserve the dignity and honor of the United States of America while under attack.

This war will go on for some time, to find the terrorists, to eliminate terrorism, to eliminate terrorists. I don't know how long it will go on, but it will go on probably for a longer time than we would like. But I hope we realize that we've already won it. We've already won the war. It's just a matter now of finishing it, and that isn't easy. And it's going to mean more sacrifices, and more lives lost. It could even mean more attacks, I don't know. But I know we won.

I knew we won because I saw within hours the reaction, first of the people of New York City, then of the people of the United States of America. I saw, within the first hours, the three firefighters who lifted the American flag up high, right within hours of the attack, while it was still life-threatening to be there, as it was for a long time. They took the American flag, and they lifted it high into the sky. And that picture was shown all over the world. And it was quite clear that we had already won when so many people came here from all over the country to help us and assist us, and came to this church, which is now used to give some relief and some help to all the people who are doing this very difficult work.

And they came here from all over the country, and the people lined up along the West Side Highway for days, day after day after day, waving the American flag, holding signs saying "We Love You," giving water to the relief workers who were going down there. The people along the West Side Highway cheered with tremendous enthusiasm for me and for George Pataki. I think four of them had voted for me, and four had voted for him. And then when they cheered for President Bush—and none of them voted for him—I knew for sure that we had won.

But as I said at the very beginning of my last discussion, my strength comes absolutely from you, and you retain it all. I come from Brooklyn. That's where I was born, that's the whole reason for my success. My father came from Manhattan and made me a Yankee fan. That's another source of my strength, and why I'm such a contrarian. My father also had to overcome the disappointment that he gave to his father and the mistakes that he made in his life. And he made sure that I wouldn't make the same mistakes. And for that I thank him forever. And my mother wasn't able to get a college education because she had to work to support a family during the Depression. So she made sure that she instilled in me tremendous love of history and reading and a tremendous thirst for learning. It's a great gift that she gave me, and it probably came out of the fact that she was deprived of being able to have the education that she wanted.

So all of you have all those strengths, the whole city does. I've lived in every part of the city—in Queens, in Brooklyn, in Manhattan, went to school in the Bronx. I never lived or worked in Staten Island, but I love it the most, and I'm going to retire there. Absolutely.

I hope that we fulfilled the pledge that we took 4 years ago, when I was inaugurated for my second term as Mayor. It's the oath the Fiorello Laguardia recited when he took the oath of office as mayor in 1934. I read just a part of it: "We will never bring disgrace to this our city, by any act of dishonesty or cowardice, nor ever desert our suffering comrades in the ranks. We will fight for our ideals and the sacred things of the city, both alone and with many. Thus in all these ways we will transmit this city, not only not less, but far greater and more beautiful than it was transmitted to us."

That's what we tried to do. And one of the ways we tried to do that was with our cultural institutions, which are at the core of what this city is all about. With the expansion of the Museum of Modern Art and the new project at Lincoln Center. You have to go take a look at the Tweed Courthouse. If we could change the name of the place—name it after some Republican. Or go look at City Hall Park, and see what it looks like now, just as a few examples of what you can do if you just kind of push through all of the things that hold you back in a city like this, for getting things accomplished. There are just too many things to talk about, and too many people to thank.

But there's one big change that's taken place that is the most important and the one that I wanted to bring about. It's the change in the spirit of the city. The city that used to be called "the rotting apple," that 70% of the people wanted to leave and nobody wanted to come to—that

city now is a very strong one, and it's a confident city. It's a city that has withstood the worst attack of any city in the history of America, and people are standing up as tall, as strong, and as straight as this church.

We're in a very holy place, and we're really on territory that is hallowed in very special ways by the presence of George Washington and all of our brave heroes that gave their lives. Never before, I don't think, in the history of America did so many people die and then end up saving so many people. It's an unbelievable thing that happened.

So I really believe we shouldn't think about the site out there, right beyond us, right here, as a site for economic development. I think we should think about it this way: We should think about how we can find the most creative minds possible who love and honor America, and can express that in artistic ways that I can't, but they can. And we should think about a soaring, monumental, beautiful memorial that draws millions of people here who just want to see it, and also those who will want to come here for reading and education and background and research.

You know, long after we're all gone, it's the sacrifice of our patriots and their heroism that is going to be what this place is remembered for. It could be a place that is remembered 100 and 1,000 years from now, like the great battlefields of Europe and of the United States. And we really have to be able to do with it what they did with Normandy or Valley Forge or Bunker Hill or Gettysburg. We have to be able to create something here that enshrines this forever and that allows people to build on it and grow from it.

And its not going to happen if we just think about it in a very narrow way. "How do you replace the offices?" "How do you get jobs?" We can do all of that. You've got to think of it from the point of view of a soaring, beautiful memorial. And then if we do that part right, then the economic development will just happen. Millions of people will come here and then we'll have all of the economic development that we want. And we can do the office space in a lot of different places.

I feel very very strongly about this, and it's something that I'm not going to forget, and its something that I'm going to continue to speak up on because I feel

that I owe that in a very, very personal way. Thousands of people died there, and hundreds of them died as rescue workers. They didn't have to go there. They walked in to try to pull people out. Some of them are very close friends of mine, and some of them are very close friends of people I love and care about, and are related to the people I love and care about. And I'm a survivor like the church is, and so are all those people sitting there. Joe Lhota, Bob Harding, Tony Coles, Rudy Washington, Neal Cohen, Bernie Kerik, Tom Von Essen, and Richard Sheirer, Tony Carbonetti, Sunny Mindel, Mike Hess, Geoff Hess, Steve Fishner, Adam Barsky. They were all with me—and Joe Dunne and Joe Esposito. Patty Verone helped to get me out and John Huvane and Freddy Garcia, Richard Godfried— who protect me—they got us out, and we survived. The building could have fallen in a different way. We could have decided to stay somewhere else, and then we wouldn't be here today.

So I think we have an obligation to the people who did die to make sure of two things about which there can be absolutely no compromise—their families need to be protected just as if they had been alive, financially and in every other way that we can help and assist their families. There should be no compromise about that ever. And second, this place has to be sanctified. This place has to become a place in which, when anybody comes here, immediately they're going to feel the great power and strength and emotion of what it means to be an American. We have to do that, and not worry about other things because this is too important a place. In their memory we have to do that.

I'm going to conclude, not with my words, but with somebody else's. On a battlefield in Pennsylvania, where a similar number of Americans died for the very same reason—to preserve our Union. A president, whose hero when he was growing up was George Washington, gave a speech, a poem, and a prayer that really says it so much better than I can say it. I'd like to read and conclude with the last part of it:

"We are met on a great battlefield of that war. We have come to dedicate a portion of that field as a final resting place for those who here gave their lives that that nation might live. It is altogether fitting and proper that we should do this. But in a larger sense we cannot dedicate, we cannot consecrate, we cannot hallow this ground. The brave men, living and dead, who struggled here, have consecrated it far above our power to add or detract. The world will little note nor long remember what we say here. But it can never forget what they did here. It is for us to live on. Rather to be dedicated here to the unfinished work that they have thus far so nobly carried on. It is rather for us to be here dedicated to the great task remaining before us. That from these honored dead, we take increased devotion to the cause for which they gave the last full measure of devotion. That we here highly resolve that the dead shall not have died in vain. That the nation shall, under God, have a new birth of freedom and the government of the people, by the people, and for the people shall not perish from this earth." God Bless New York and God Bless America.

Thomas Von Essen, New York's fire chief, former Mayor Giuliani, and New York Police Chief Bernard Kerik after they received their honorary awards at Buckingham Palace in central London on February 13 from Britain's Queen Elizabeth II. Giuliani became an Honorary Knight Commander, while Von Essen and Kerik received honorary Commander of the British Empire medals.

The former Mayor Giuliani holds one of his pictures of the Twin Towers up for auction, at the Royal Academy of Arts in London. The former mayor and other celebrities were at the academy to attend an auction to raise money for the dependents of the firemen and policemen killed in the attacks. Mr. Giuliani donated some of his own personal photos of the city, which raised several thousand dollars.

World Leaders Unite

President Bush confers with French President Jacques Chirac (left) in the Oval Office of the White House on September 18 in Washington, D.C. Chirac affirmed that Paris was determined to support Washington's war on the "absolute evil" of terrorism.

President Chirac Pledges Support

PRESIDENT BUSH: It is my honor to welcome a good friend, a good personal friend and a good friend of America to the Oval Office. It's the first formal visit I've had with any world leader since the terrible day a week ago.

After the incident, after that day, I got a lot of phone calls, and one of the most meaningful phone calls of all was from Jacques Chirac, who expressed his concern for the American citizens. He expressed his desire to stand solidly with America during this terrible, terrible day.

President Chirac understands that we have entered a new type of war. It's a war against people who hate freedom. And I am honored to welcome our friend here to the Oval Office.

Welcome, sir.

PRESIDENT CHIRAC: Thank you. I've come here to tell you of the emotion—the emotion of France, the French people, an emotion which has no precedent in history before this tragedy, which does not have a parallel. Indeed, it is a tragic event, something which is beyond crime; there are no words to qualify it.

I want to tell President Bush, who is my friend, that we stand in total solidarity—we bring you the total solidarity of France and the French people. It is solidarity of the heart.

I also wanted to say that we are completely determined to fight by your side this new type of evil, of absolute evil, which is terrorism. And I also wanted to say that France is prepared and available to discuss all means to fight and eradicate this evil.

PRESIDENT BUSH: Thank you, sir.

British Premier Tony Blair (left) and German Chancellor Gerhard Schroeder address the media during a press conference after their meeting in Berlin on September 19. Blair and Schroeder met to discuss further diplomatic and military steps in fighting international terrorism following terrorist attacks in the U.S. last week.

British Prime Minister Tony Blair and President Bush speak to the press at the White House on September 20 before the President was to deliver his address to the Congress on his plans for war against terrorism.

President Bush meets with Kingdom of Saudi Arabia's Foreign Minister Saud al-Faisal (left) on September 20 in the Oval Office. The two met to discuss U.S. plans for a war on terrorism in the aftermath of the September 11 terrorist attacks.

136

REMARKS BY THE PRESIDENT AND PRIME
MINISTER CHRETIEN OF CANADA
THE COLONNADE

THE PRESIDENT: It's my honor to welcome our close friend, Jean Chretien, to the White House again. Thank you for coming.

You know, after this terrible incident on September 11th, one of the first phone calls I received was from the Prime Minister, offering all his support and condolences to the United States and our citizens. It was like getting a phone call from a brother. And I appreciate that so very much.

We've got a great partner in our neighborhood who understands what I know, that we are facing a new type of war. And those of us who love freedom, like the Canadians love freedom, now understand that freedom is under attack. And we've combined together to fight— to fight against a new enemy. And the Prime Minister understands that.

We had a great discussion about a variety of issues. We discussed the need for us to continue to work peacefully along a huge border. Border relations between Canada and Mexico have never been better. And there is no doubt in my mind that the Prime Minister and the Canadian people will work hard to make sure that Canada is secure from any terrorist activity that takes place, just like I can assure the Prime Minister we're doing the same. We both have a mutual responsibility in our hemisphere to find and disrupt terrorist organizations.

An amazing thing came up the other day. Somebody said to me, well, you know, in your speech to Congress, there were some that took affront in Canada because I didn't mention the name. I didn't necessarily think it was important to praise a brother; after all, we're talking about family.

There should be no doubt in anybody's mind about how honored we are to have the support of the Canadians, and how strong the Canadian Prime Minister has been. And not only his condolences, but his offer of support for the American people. I guess there's—somebody is playing politics with you, Mr. Prime Minister.

But I suggest those who try to play politics with my words and drive wedges between

Canadian Prime Minister Jean Chretien (left) speaks to the press as President Bush looks on at the White House Rose Garden on September 24.

Canada and me, understand that at this time, when nations are under attack, now is not the time for politics. Now is the time to develop a strategy to fight and win the war. And Mr. Prime Minister, I want to thank you for being here to continue those efforts with me.

PRIME MINISTER CHRETIEN: Thank you, Mr. President. And I am happy to be with you. I think that, as you say, we're part of—not America, we're your neighbor, friends and family. And we have to work together. This problem of terrorism is a problem that concerns

all the nations of the world. And we're working together to build a coalition that will defeat that, because it will disrupt the societies around the world. And I think that you know you have the support of Canadians. When you will need us, we will be there.

We had a very good discussion this morning on the element of the solutions and we will carry on during the lunch time. I guess that the Canadians were traumatized by what happened two weeks ago.

President Bush and Japanese Prime Minister Junichiro Koizumi (left) speak with the media in the White House Rose Garden on September 25 in Washington, D.C. The two discussed Japan's participation in the U.S. coalition to combat global terrorism.

The emir of Qatar, Sheik Hamad bin Khalifa Al-Thani (left), shakes hands with New York City Mayor Rudolph Giuliani (center) as New York Police Commissioner Bernard Kerik looks on at the World Trade Center disaster command center in New York on October 2. His Highness made a donation of one million dollars to the Twin Towers fund and one million dollars to the Widows' and Children's fund for the New York Fire Department.

President Bush shakes hands with King Abdullah II of Jordan (left) in the Oval Office on September 28. Bush and King Abdullah II met in support of the U.S. counterterrorism campaign.

REMARKS BY PRESIDENT BUSH AND HIS MAJESTY KING ABDULLAH OF JORDAN

PRESIDENT BUSH: Your Majesty, welcome back.

KING ABDULLAH: Thank you.

PRESIDENT BUSH: It's great to see you. I look forward to our discussions. Jordan is a strong, strong friend of America. And right after September 11th, one of the early messages I received was from His Majesty, expressing the condolences of the Jordanian people, as well as his own personal condolences.

I'm so pleased with our cooperative—the cooperation we have in fighting terror. I have assured His Majesty that our war is against evil, not against Islam. There are thousands of Muslims who proudly call themselves Americans, and they know what I know—that the Muslim faith is based upon peace and love and compassion. The exact opposite of the teachings of the al Qaeda organization, which is based upon evil and hate and destruction.

And finally, as a welcoming gift, it is my honor to present you with a pen. This is no ordinary pen, since it's the pen I used to sign the Free Trade Agreement with Jordan this morning. At long last, we have, together, accomplished one of your main objectives in terms of economic cooperation, which is the Free Trade Agreement.

I'm proud of the actions of our leadership in the House and the Senate from both political parties that recognize the importance of trade with Jordan. And so, Your Majesty, it's now officially the law, and here's the pen that signed it.

KING ABDULLAH: Thank you very much, sir. Very grateful.

PRESIDENT BUSH: Welcome back to the Oval Office.

KING ABDULLAH: Sir, I would like to take this opportunity to thank you for seeing us today. Obviously, I wish our meeting was under better circumstances, but obviously, we're here to give our full, unequivocal support to you and to the people of America. And we will stand by you in these very difficult times. And we're proud of our friendship; we're proud of the relations we've had with your country over many, many years, as far back as his late Majesty King Hussein.

And it's in difficult times like this that true friends must stand with each other, and we'll be by your side and we'll be there to support you. And I'm here to see what we can do to help.

PRESIDENT BUSH: Thank you, sir.

Britain's Prime Minister Tony Blair (left) meets Russian President Vladimir Putin on October 4. Mr Blair's visit to Russia and meeting with the Russian president is part of the coalition-building process to identify those responsible for the attacks on the U.S. on September 11th.

PRESIDENT FOX REAFFIRMS COMMITMENT TO U.S.

PRESIDENT BUSH: It is my honor to welcome my friend back to the White House. It wasn't all that long ago that we were standing out here for the opening ceremony of the first and only state dinner I've had since I've been the President. He came as a friend then, and he's come back as a loyal friend to the United States.

September 11th really changed America. President Fox understood that right off the bat. One of the first calls I got was from Vicente Fox. He called expressing his deep condolences to the American people. He was very kind to me. He wished me well. President Fox understands that an attack on America affects Mexico in a significant way. After all, there are millions of Mexican Americans and Mexican nationals living in America; men and women who saw a land they love attacked; men and women who have united around a great cause of defending freedom.

In this country we don't ask the question, what is your religion or where are you from. We ask the question, are you united to defend freedom. And there are millions of Mexican Americans who understand that call. So when the President said, we stand with you, he is not only saying, we stand with the United States government, he's saying, we stand with millions of people living in our country, as well.

President Fox and I had a great discussion about ways we can continue to cooperate. We need to cooperate on security matters along our border, which we are. We need to continue working on other agenda items that we have been working on, and we will.

Obviously, our nation is now focused on the incidents of September 11th. But I assured him our relationship will go forward, that we'll work on the issues that we had discussed the last time we were here. I talked to my friend about our economy. It has been affected significantly by the actions of September the 11th.

But I assured him that we will take an aggressive role at the federal level to try to spur economic growth, which is very important, since we've got a significant amount of trade between our nations.

In sum, I'm so glad he came back. It's comforting to know that our friend to the south is going to be a friend in good times and in tough times.

So, Mr. President, welcome back. Thank you for coming.

PRESIDENT FOX: Thank you. And thank you, President, for the opportunity to be back here again; the opportunity to express very clearly, loudly, our sorrow, our solidarity with your government, with the American people, with the victims and all those who suffered under these attacks. But also, the opportunity to reaffirm our commitments.

We are a friend, we are neighbors, we are partners, and we want to make very clear that this means commitment all the way, and that we will keep our commitments.

And we are working on an everyday basis, either in the border, either in customs, either in migration, either—on each of the subjects that have to do with security. We will be side by side in your efforts to defeat terrorism in the world and wherever it is.

We will be coordinating, participating, collaborating on our side with our resources that we have at hand. And we know of your efforts not only to meet this challenge, we know the efforts also to keep America moving. And that's something that we very proudly see, that this nation does not know about defeat; on the contrary. But it's working to come back to be the leader, to be that strong spirit and economy that is an example for all of us.

And we're working in the same direction. We know that in economic terms, things are interactive; as well, as we buy a lot of products, services from the United States, we sell a lot of products to the United States, being one of the largest trading two economies in the world. And through working in that direction, we can also contribute to overcoming this situation.

So, thanks again for giving us this opportunity. And we go back knowing that we have a lot of work to do, that we've been doing and that we will keep on doing. So, thank you, President.

PRESIDENT BUSH: Thank you, Mr. President.

New York City Mayor Rudolph Giuliani (right) greets Mexican President Vicente Fox (left) at the Pier 92 Command Center in New York City on October 4. Fox toured the area of the devastation from the attacks on the World Trade Center, and underlined his government's support for the global antiterror campaign during meetings with President Bush at the White House and with UN Secretary-General Kofi Annan in New York.

141

PRESIDENT THANKS GEORGIAN PRESIDENT FOR SUPPORT AGAINST TERRORISM

During a meeting with President of Georgia Eduard Shevardnadze, President Bush underscored the continued support of the United States for the sovereignty, independence, and territorial integrity of Georgia. President Bush also thanked President Shevardnadze for Georgia's unequivocal offer of support in the campaign against international terrorism. President Bush expressed the willingness of the United States to work with Georgia to support Georgian efforts to take steps against terrorists.

Both presidents agreed on the importance of Georgia strengthening itself internally through economic and democratic reform, and a robust fight against corruption. Progress on these reforms will maintain and strengthen the partnership between the United States and Georgia as they seek to fight terrorism, promote regional cooperation and stability, and advance Caspian energy projects.

Georgian President Eduard Shevardnadze (left) and President Bush meet in the Oval Office of the White House on October 5. Shevardnadze is on a three-day visit to Washington to discuss the U.S. war on terrorism.

Turkish Prime Minister Bulent Ecevit (center, left) and Foreign Minister Ismail Cem (center, right) talk to media on at a press conference on October 7 after they summoned the government ministers to a crisis meeting shortly after the U.S. and British attacks started in Afghanistan, including strikes against Kandahar and the capital Kabul. Turkey, a faithful U.S. ally and the only Muslim member of NATO, has offered to let U.S. forces use its military bases and airspace for any attacks against Afghanistan's ruling Taliban.

Polish President Aleksander Kwasniewski makes a statement in Warsaw, October 7. Kwasniewski expressed full support for the attacks on targets in Afghanistan and in the war against terrorism

British Prime Minister Tony Blair (right) is escorted by unidentified persons as he arrives at the Hotel Intercontinental in Geneva for a meeting with the President of the United Arab Emirates Sheikh Zayed bin Sultan Al Nahyan on October 9. The meeting will be dedicated to the situation in Afghanistan.

President Bush and German Chancellor Gerhard Schroeder talk with reporters in the Rose Garden at the White House on October 9. Bush praised German Chancellor Gerhard Schroeder's support since the September 11th strikes on the United States, saying he had "no more steadfast friend" in the global war on terrorism.

GERMAN LEADER REITERATES SOLIDARITY WITH U.S.

THE PRESIDENT: It's been my honor to welcome a great friend of America to the Oval Office again. Chancellor Schroeder came to talk about our war against terrorist activities. We had a great discussion.

First, I want to thank the Chancellor for his solidarity with the American people and his strong statement of support for the American people right after the evildoers struck on September the 11th. I also want to thank Chancellor Schroeder and the German people for their outpouring of support for the victims.

And I also want to thank him for being a steadfast friend in a broad coalition that is determined to rout terrorism out where it may exist, to not only bring the al Qaeda organization to justice, but to declare a broad campaign against terrorists and terrorism all across the world.

There is no more steadfast friend in this coalition than Germany, and I'm proud to have him here. We also talked about the Middle East and the importance that both of us recognize for that process, to

get into Mitchell as quickly as possible. The German government has been very strong about working with both parties in the Middle East to get into Mitchell.

I assured him we're doing the same thing. There would be no better stabilizer for our coalition than for the Mitchell process to begin in the Middle East. But, Mr. Chancellor, we're so thrilled to have you here. Thank you for coming.

CHANCELLOR SCHROEDER: Thank you very much, indeed, Mr. President. I obviously, very happily, came here and I'm pleased to be here, because it is important to us to show that very much in these difficult times, friendship must prevail and does prevail. And I'm also here to express the deepest solidarity from the German side, which is not just words being said, but it's a fact.

We very much are in agreement about the fact that this fight against terrorism, which we are all involved in by now, must be a very comprehensive approach, indeed. The action that is being taken right now must be added to through political measures, through diplomatic action, too. We also find it very important to maintain

the strong degree of cohesion that we see at this point in time within the antiterror alliance that has formed around the world. We went on to agree that it was crucially important to dry up the financing for the terrorists, and we also find it very important to highlight that the action that is presently being taken in Afghanistan is not at all directed against the people of Afghanistan, it is not at all directed against Islam; it is far, rather, directed against Osama bin Laden and the very ruthless regime behind him.

We have also very strongly emphasized how important we find it that we do provide relief for the refugees and cope with the refugee problem that will arise. And I can only yet again emphasize the high degree of respect that I feel, vis-a-vis the United States of America and the American President, how he has gone about linking humanitarian aid and assistance with the strike in this fantastic way he has done.

THE PRESIDENT: Thank you, sir.

British Prime Minister Tony Blair (left) is greeted by the Sultan of Oman Qaboos bin Said Al-Said in his palace in Muscat on October 11.

British Prime Minister Tony Blair is greeted by Egyptian President Mubarak in Cairo on October 11.

British Prime Minister Tony Blair (right) and Danish Prime Minister Poul Nyrup Rasmussen stand on the doorstep of No.10 Downing Street, central London, following a meeting to discuss the current situation in Afghanistan.

U.S., CHINA STAND AGAINST TERRORISM

PRESIDENT JIANG: Mr. President, ladies and gentlemen, I've just had a very good talk with President Bush. This is our first meeting, and we have had an in-depth exchange of views and reached a series of consensus with respect to such major issues as Sino-U.S. relations, counterterrorism, and maintenance of world peace and stability.

China and the United States are two countries with significant influence in the world. As such, we share common responsibility and interest in maintaining peace and security in the Asia Pacific and the world at large, promoting regional and global economic growth and prosperity, and working together with the rest of the international community to combat terrorism.

China attaches importance to its relations with the United States and stands ready to make joint efforts with the U.S. side to develop a constructive and cooperative relationship.

We live in a world of diversity. Given the differences in national conditions, it is not surprising that there are certain disagreements between China and the United States. I believe that different civilizations and social systems ought to have long-term coexistence and achieve common development in the spirit of seeking common ground while shelving differences.

The Sino-U.S. relations are currently faced with the important opportunities of development. We will conduct high-level strategic dialogue, advance exchanges in cooperation in economic, trade, energy, and other fields, and strengthen consultation and coordination on major international and regional issues.

I'm confident that so long as the two sides keep a firm hold of the common interests of the two countries, properly handled, bilateral ties, especially the question of Taiwan, in accordance with the three Sino-U.S. joint communiques, the relations between China and the United States will continuously move forward.

President Bush and Chinese President Jiang Zemin (right) react at the Western Suburb Guest House in Shanghai, China, on October 19. Bush is in Shanghai to attend the APEC Summit.

PRESIDENT BUSH: Mr. President, thank you very much. I, too, felt like we had a very good meeting. I've come to Shanghai because China and other Asia Pacific nations are important partners in the global coalition against terror.

I've also come because the economic future of my nation and this region are inseparable. The nations of APEC share the same threat, and we share the same hope for greater trade and prosperity.

Thank you so much for hosting this meeting. You and the city of Shanghai have done an outstanding job. Mr. President, I visited this city 25 years ago—a little over 25 years ago. Then I could not have imagined the dynamic and impressive Shanghai of 2001. It's an impressive place, and I know you're proud. It's a tribute to the leadership of the current officials of Shanghai, as well as to your leadership as a former mayor, Mr. President.

We have a common understanding of the magnitude of the threat posed by international terrorism. All civilized nations must join together to defeat this threat. And I believe that the United States and China can accomplish a lot when we work together to fight terrorism. The President and the government of China responded immediately to the attacks of September 11th. There was no hesitation, there was no doubt that they would stand with the United States and our people during this terrible time. There is a firm commitment by this government to cooperate in intelligence matters, to help interdict financing of terrorist organizations. It is—President Jiang and the government stand side by side with the American people as we fight this evil force.

China is a great power. And America wants a constructive relationship with China. We welcome a China that is a full member of world community, that is at peace with its neighbors. We welcome and support China's accession into the World Trade Organization. We believe it's a very important development that will benefit our two peoples and the world.

In the long run, the advance of Chinese prosperity depends on China's full integration into the rules and norms of international institutions. And in the long run, economic freedom and political freedom will go hand in hand.

We've had a very broad discussion, including the fact that the war on terrorism must never be an excuse to persecute minorities. I explained my views on Taiwan and preserving regional stability in East Asia. I stressed the need to combat the proliferation of weapons of mass destruction and missile technology.

Today's meetings convinced me that we can build on our common interests. Two great nations will rarely agree on everything; I understand that. But I assured the President that we'll always deal with our differences in a spirit of mutual respect. We seek a relationship that is candid, constructive and cooperative.

I leave my country at a very difficult time. But this meeting is important because of the campaign against terror, because of the ties between two great nations, because the opportunity and hope that trade provides for both our people.

I regret, Mr. President, I couldn't accept your invitation to visit Beijing, but it will happen at a different time.

PRESIDENT JIANG: Next time.

PRESIDENT BUSH: That's right. Thank you for your hospitality.

President Bush shakes hands with Korean President Kim Dae Jung at the Portman Ritz-Carlton in Shanghai, China, on October 19.

Prince Albert of Monaco (left) listens to Richard Sheirer, director of the Office of Emergency Management, during his visit to ground zero in New York on October 23. Prince Albert presented Mayor Rudolph Giuliani a check for $710,000 from the principality to a fund for relatives of police, firefighters, and other emergency workers killed in the hijacked plane attacks on New York prior to his visit to ground zero.

Venezuela's President Hugo Chavez (right) is greeted by British Prime Minister Tony Blair at No.10 Downing Street in London on October 23. Chavez is in Britain on a three-day visit.

President Bush shakes hands with Crown Prince Sheikh Salman bin Hamad Al-Khalifa (left) of Bahrain before their meeting on October 25 at the White House.

Israeli Prime Minister Ariel Sharon (right) listens to his British counterpart Tony Blair during a press conference at the end of a working lunch on November 1 at the Prime Minister's residence in Jerusalem. Blair arrived in Israel on an official visit, meeting with Israelis and Palestinians leaders to try to solve the stalemate in the Middle East peace process.

President Bush enjoys a laugh with the President of Nigeria Olusegun Obasanjo (left) on the steps outside the Oval Office of the White House on November 2. Bush and Obasanjo discussed bilateral relations between the countries.

PRESIDENT MEETS WITH PRIME MINISTER OF INDIA

THE PRESIDENT: Mr. Prime Minister, welcome to the United States. It's my honor to welcome the Prime Minister of India to the White House for a series of discussions. My administration is committed to developing a fundamentally different relationship with India, one based upon trust, one based upon mutual values. After all, the Prime Minister leads a nation that is the largest democratic nation in the world...We will fight terrorism together. Our initial discussions focused on the battle against terror, and the Prime Minister understands that we have no option but to win. And he understands that there is a commitment—there needs to be a commitment by all of us to do more than just talk. It's to achieve certain objectives—to cut off the finances, to put diplomatic pressure on the terrorists, in some cases, to help militarily. But, in any case, stand firm in the face of terror... So, Mr. Prime Minister, I am extremely

optimistic about our relationship. It's an important relationship for our country. And I welcome you to the United States. Thank you for coming.

PRIME MINISTER VAJPAYEE: Thank you, Mr. President, for your kinds words. It is a pleasure to be here to continue the practice of regular dialogue that India and the USA have established in recent years.
I was happy to be able to personally reiterate our sympathy, solidarity and support for the American people in the aftermath of terrible events of September 11th.
We admire the decisive leadership of President Bush in the international coalition against terrorism. We also applaud the resilience and resolve of the American people in this hour of trial. This terrible tragedy has created the opportunity to fashion a determined global response to terrorism in all its forms and manifestations, wherever it exists and under whatever name. I assured President Bush of India's complete support in this.

President Bush and Indian Prime Minister Atal Vajpayee (left) hold a joint press conference at the White House on November 9 in Washington, D.C. Bush and Vajpayee met earlier in the Oval Office to discuss the war in Afghanistan.

At the same time, as material leaders, pluralist democracies, we should clearly spread the message that the war against terrorism is not against any religion, but against terrorists whose propaganda misuses religion...Thank you.

JOINT STATEMENT FOR THE VISIT OF PAKISTANI PRESIDENT PERVEZ MUSHARRAF TO NEW YORK

President George W. Bush and President Pervez Musharraf met in New York today and reaffirmed the strength and vitality of the bilateral relationship between Pakistan and the United States. The two Presidents expressed the conviction that the global coalition against terrorism is essential for the elimination of the Taliban regime and the al Qaeda network and those who harbor them. President Musharraf welcomed the clear commitments expressed by President Bush to continued active United States engagement in Pakistan and the entire South Asian sub-continent.

President Bush and President Musharraf reaffirmed the benefits of 50 years of friendship and close cooperation between Pakistan and the United States and recalled the pivotal role of the Pakistan-U.S. alliance in the triumph of the free world at the end of the cold war. They

welcomed the revival of this longstanding partnership and expressed their conviction that it would constitute a vital element in the construction of a durable structure of peace, stability, economic growth, and enhanced prosperity at the regional and global level. They also held wide-ranging discussions on the current antiterrorism campaign and exchanged views on bilateral, regional, and international issues.

President Musharraf strongly condemned the terrorist attacks of September 11 and conveyed the sympathy and solidarity of the people and government of Pakistan to the people and government of the United States. President Bush recognized Pakistan's role as a front-line state in the global campaign against terrorism and expressed gratitude for Pakistan's vital support in the international campaign. Both leaders agreed to continue their ongoing excellent cooperation and to pursue a coherent and coordinated diplomatic, political, military, economic, financial and humanitarian strategy

Pakistan President Pervez Musharraf (left) and President Bush hold a joint press conference on November 10 at the Waldorf-Astoria Hotel in New York. Musharraf said there were signs that the US-Pakistan relationship, which had distanced in recent years, was regaining its momentum.

to eliminate terrorism…They agreed that the United States and Pakistan can accomplish great things together and that the American and Pakistani people look forward to building peace, stability and prosperity, both in South Asia and around the world.

153

Russian President Vladimir Putin (left) and President Bush smile following a press conference at Crawford High School in Crawford, Texas, on November 15. Presidents Putin and Bush spoke about their meeting at the Bush ranch.

PRESIDENT ANNOUNCES REDUCTION IN NUCLEAR ARSENAL

PRESIDENT BUSH: It's a great honor for me to welcome President Vladimir Putin to the White House, and to welcome his wife as well. This is a new day in the long history of Russian-American relations, a day of progress and a day of hope.

The United States and Russia are in the midst of a transformation of a relationship that will yield peace and progress. We're transforming our relationship from one of hostility and suspicion to one based on cooperation and trust, that will enhance opportunities for peace and progress for our citizens and for people all around the world.

The challenge of terrorism makes our close cooperation on all issues even more urgent. Russia and America share the same threat and the same resolve. We will fight and defeat terrorist networks wherever they exist. Our highest priority is to keep terrorists from acquiring weapons of mass destruction.

Today, we agreed that Russian and American experts will work together to share information and expertise to counter the threat from bioterrorism. We agreed that it is urgent that we improve the physical protection and accounting of nuclear materials and prevent illicit nuclear trafficking.

And we will strengthen our efforts to cut off every possible source of biological, chemical and nuclear weapons, materials and expertise. Today, we also agreed to work more closely to combat organized crime and drug-trafficking, a leading source of terrorist financing.

Both nations are committed to the reconstruction of Afghanistan, once hostilities there have ceased and the Taliban are no longer in control. We support the UN's efforts to fashion a post-Taliban government that is broadly based and multi-ethnic. The new government must export neither terror nor drugs, and it must respect fundamental human rights.

And Russia and the United States—as Russia and the United States work more closely to meet new 21st century threats, we're also working hard to put the threats of the 20th century behind us once and for all.

I want to thank President Putin for the spirit of our meetings. Together, we're making history, as we make progress. Laura and I are looking forward to welcoming the Putins to our ranch in Crawford, Texas. I can't wait to show you my state, and where I live. In the meantime, I hope you have a fine stay here in Washington, D.C. And it's my honor to welcome you to the White House, sir, and welcome you to the podium.

PRESIDENT PUTIN: Ladies and gentlemen, I don't know whether I would have an opportunity to address such a representative audience of the press and media. I would like to begin, anyway, with a thanks to the President of the United States, not only for his kind invitation to visit the United States and Washington, but also for his very informal initiation of our negotiations earlier today. Myself and my colleagues are very pleased to be here, this historic building of the White House. And President Bush deemed it appropriate not only to tour me, to guide me through the premises of this house, where he lives, he—saw almost every picture hanging on the walls of this great building.

It's not only very interesting, but it is not only very interesting, but it also changes for the better the quality of our relationship.

I would like to once again thank the President and the American people, and I would like to express our condolences in connection with the recent plane crash in the United States. As they say in Russia, tragedy does not come alone. And tragedies always come in many numbers. I am confident that the U.S.—American people would face this tragedy very bravely.

I would like to inform you that the Washington part of our negotiations is being completed and our discussions proved very constructive, interesting, and useful and will continue at Crawford. But the preliminary results we evaluate as extremely positive.

This is our fourth meeting with President Bush in the last few months. I believe this is a vivid demonstration of the dynamic nature of the Russian-American relations. We have come to understand each other better and our positions are becoming closer on the key issues of bilateral and international relations.

We are prepared now to seek solutions in all areas of our joint activities. We intend to dismantle conclusively the vestiges of the Cold War and to develop new—entirely new partnership for long term.

Of course, we discussed in detail the subject matter of fight against terrorism. The tragic developments of September 11th demonstrated vividly the need for a joint effort to counter this global threat. We consider this threat as a global threat, indeed, and the terrorists and those who help them should know that the justice is inescapable and it will reach them, wherever they try to hide.

Also, post-crisis political settlement in Afghanistan was discussed. The most important thing for today is to return peace and the life and honor to Afghanistan, so that no threat originate from Afghanistan to the international stability. Of course, we do not intend to force upon the Afghani people the solutions; it is for them to resolve those issues with the active participation of the United Nations.

We also exchanged on a number of topical issues of international importance: the Balkans, Iraq, and we reiterated in a joint statement the resolve of the United States and Russia to facilitate settlement in the Middle East and the early resumption of negotiations between Israelis and Palestinians…Direct contacts are expanding between entrepreneurs of the two countries, including within the Russian-American business dialogue. It is with satisfaction that we note a certain progress in issues related to the Russia's accession to the WTO. In recognizing Russia as a market economy country, and we've felt a great degree of understanding that such issues should be resolved, I mean, dealing with the Jackson-Vanik amendment, not de facto, but in legal terms. And in this context, our Foreign Minister and the Secretary of State, Messrs. Ivanov and Powell exchanged letters reiterating the resolve of Russia and the United States to observe human rights and religious freedoms.

Of course, the capabilities imbedded in the bilateral relationship have not been fully implemented. The key—we have quite a lot of things to do, but we are confident that the success is by and large predetermined by our resolve to cooperate energetically and constructively. That, and I'm confident, would benefit both countries. And which is reflected, also, in our visit to this country today.

Thank you.

President Bush (left) makes remarks at a luncheon hosted by UN Secretary-General Kofi Annan (second from left) and joined by Brazilian President Fernando Henrique Cardoso (second from right) and Pakistani President Pervez Musharraf on November 10 at the United Nations.

President Bush stands at attention with Ambassador of the Republic of Nigeria Jibril Aminu, Ambassador of the Republic of Korea Sung Chul Yang, and Ambassador of the Republic of Turkey Faruk Logoglu during ceremonies at the White House commemorating the sixth-month anniversary of the September 11 terrorist attacks against the United States.

President Bush has a joint press conference with Interim Afghan leader Hamid Karzai in the White House Rose Garden on January 28, 2002, in Washington, D.C. Karzai is on his first official visit to Washington and will appear as an honored guest of President Bush at the State of the Union address.

President Bush (center) and Prime Minister of Ireland Bertie Ahern (left) are escorted down the stairs outside the U.S. Capitol by the Speaker of the House, Dennis Hartert (right), in front of bagpipers on March 13, 2002.

Attacking the Taliban

Afghan opposition fighters do exercises at the military training camp of the Hazati Mahamed's division near Jabal os Saraje, on October 1. The countdown to conflict in Afghanistan was ticking faster with a U.S. warning that the Taliban's days in power were numbered and the ruling Islamic militia threatening a protracted guerrilla war.

OPERATION ENDURING FREEDOM OVERVIEW

- Russia offered to share information and the use of their airspace for humanitarian flights.
- China offered to share information.
- India offered to share information and pledged support of U.S. actions.
- Japan offered diplomatic and military (logistical) support, and assistance to Pakistan.
- Australia offered combat military forces and invoked Article IV of the ANZUS Treaty, declaring September 11 an attack on Australia.
- South Korea offered military medical and air and naval logistics support.
- UAE and Saudi Arabia broke diplomatic relations with the Taliban.
- Pakistan agreed to cooperate fully with the request for assistance and support.
- Secured overflight and landing rights from 27 countries.
- Obtained 46 multilateral declarations of support.
- Nineteen nations of NATO invoked Article V declaring an attack on one as an attack on all.

- The United Nations Security Council unanimously enacted a binding resolution requiring all member states to pursue terrorists and those who support them, including financial support systems.

DEPARTMENT OF THE TREASURY:

- Adoption of Terrorist Financing Executive Order.
- Froze approximately 30 al Qaeda accounts in the U.S. and almost 20 overseas.
- Put 27 names on the Terrorist Financing list.
- Reviewing additional persons and entities for possible inclusion on the Terrorist Financing list.
- Froze approximately $6 million linked to terrorists.

DEPARTMENT OF DEFENSE:

- Approximately 29,000 military personnel, 349 military aircraft, 1 Amphibious Ready Group, and 2 Carrier Battle Groups currently deployed in Theater.
- Approximately 17,000 members of the reserve have been called to active duty, as well as several thousand National Guard operating under State authority.

- Department of Justice:
- Analyzed 241 serious/credible threats.
- Conducted 540 interviews.
- Conducted 383 searches.
- Issued 4,407 subpoenas.
- Arrested/Detained 439 persons.
- Approximately 30-plus countries offered support in criminal investigations.

INTELLIGENCE:

- Over 100 countries have offered increased intelligence support.
- Approximately 150 arrests and detentions of terrorists and suspected supporters of terrorism in over 25 countries.
- Intensified counterterrorist operations with over 200 intelligence and security services worldwide.

An F-14 Tomcat and an F/A-18 Hornet aircraft assigned to the aircraft carrier USS Enterprise complete air-to-air refueling operations with a U.S. Air Force KC-10 Extender from the 763rd Expeditionary Air Refueling Squadron on October 5. The refueling squadron supports Navy jets conducting missions in support of Operation Enduring Freedom.

President George W. Bush announces that U.S. Armed Forces have begun a bombing campaign of Afghanistan on Sunday, October 7. The U.S. launched attacks against Afghanistan as a new front in its war on terrorism.

Secretary of Defense Donald Rumsfeld (right) and Chairman of the Joint Chiefs of Staff General Richard Myers brief the press on October 7 in the Pentagon about U.S. air strikes on Taliban positions in Afghanistan

This photo released by the Department of Defense shows aviation ordnance men moving a 1,000 pound bomb onto the flight deck of the aircraft carrier USS Carl Vinson in preparation for strikes against al Qaeda terrorist training camps and military installations of the Taliban regime in Afghanistan on October 7.

A Tomahawk cruise missile takes off from the USS Philippine Sea on October 7. Retaliatory strikes against Afghanistan began October 7 in the first stage of the campaign against the Taliban regime for sheltering Saudi-born alleged terrorism mastermind Osama bin Laden, who is the "prime suspect" in the September 11 attacks in the U.S.

ATTACKING THE TALIBAN

THE PRESIDENT: Good afternoon. On my orders, the United States military has begun strikes against al Qaeda terrorist training camps and military installations of the Taliban regime in Afghanistan. These carefully targeted actions are designed to disrupt the use of Afghanistan as a terrorist base of operations, and to attack the military capability of the Taliban regime.

We are joined in this operation by our staunch friend, Great Britain. Other close friends, including Canada, Australia, Germany, and France, have pledged forces as the operation unfolds. More than 40 countries in the Middle East, Africa, Europe, and across Asia have granted air transit or landing rights. Many more have shared intelligence. We are supported by the collective will of the world.

More than two weeks ago, I gave Taliban leaders a series of clear and specific demands: Close terrorist training camps, hand over leaders of the al Qaeda network, and return all foreign nationals, including American citizens, unjustly detained in your country. None of these demands were met. And now the Taliban will pay a price. By destroying camps and disrupting communications, we will make it more difficult for the terror network to train new recruits and coordinate their evil plans.

Initially, the terrorists may burrow deeper into caves and other entrenched hiding places. Our military action is also designed to clear the way for sustained, comprehensive, and relentless operations to drive them out and bring them to justice.

At the same time, the oppressed people of Afghanistan will know the generosity of America and our allies. As we strike military targets, we'll also drop food, medicine, and supplies to the starving and suffering men and women and children of Afghanistan.

The United States of America is a friend to the Afghan people, and we are the friends of almost a billion worldwide who practice the Islamic faith. The United States of America is an enemy of those who aid terrorists and of the barbaric criminals who profane a great religion by committing murder in its name.

This military action is a part of our campaign against terrorism, another front in a war that has already been joined through diplomacy, intelligence, the freezing of financial assets, and the arrests of known terrorists by law enforcement agents in 38 countries. Given the nature and reach of our enemies, we will win this conflict by the patient accumulation of successes, by meeting a series of challenges with determination, and will and purpose.

Today we focus on Afghanistan, but the battle is broader. Every nation has a choice to make. In this conflict, there is no neutral ground. If any government sponsors the outlaws and killers of innocents, they have become outlaws and murderers, themselves. And they will take that lonely path at their own peril.

I'm speaking to you today from the Treaty Room of the White House, a place where American presidents have worked for peace. We're a peaceful nation. Yet, as we have learned, so suddenly and so tragically, there can be no peace in a world of sudden terror. In the face of today's new threat, the only way to pursue peace is to pursue those who threaten it.

We did not ask for this mission, but we will fulfill it. The name of today's military operation is Enduring Freedom. We defend not only our precious freedoms, but also the freedom of people everywhere to live and raise their children free from fear.

I know many Americans feel fear today. And our government is taking strong precautions. All law enforcement and intelligence agencies are working aggressively around America, around the world, and around the clock. At my request, many governors have activated the National Guard to strengthen airport security. We have called up reserves to reinforce our military capability and strengthen the protection of our homeland.

In the months ahead, our patience will be one of our strengths—patience with the long waits that will result from tighter security, patience and understanding that it will take time to achieve our goals, patience in all the sacrifices that may come.

Today, those sacrifices are being made by members of our Armed Forces who now defend us so far from home, and by their proud and worried families. A Commander-in-Chief sends America's sons and daughters into a battle in a foreign land only after the greatest care and a lot of prayer. We ask a lot of those who wear our uniform. We ask them to leave their loved ones, to travel great distances, to risk injury, even to be prepared to make the ultimate sacrifice of their lives. They are dedicated, they are honorable; they represent the best of our country. And we are grateful.

To all the men and women in our military—every sailor, every soldier, every airman, every coastguardsman, every Marine—I say this: Your mission is defined; your objectives are clear; your goal is just. You have my full confidence, and you will have every tool you need to carry out your duty.

I recently received a touching letter that says a lot about the state of America in these difficult times—a letter from a fourth-grade girl, with a father in the military: "As much as I don't want my dad to fight," she wrote, "I'm willing to give him to you."

This is a precious gift, the greatest she could give. This young girl knows what America is all about. Since September 11, an entire generation of young Americans has gained new understanding of the value of freedom, and its cost in duty and in sacrifice.

The battle is now joined on many fronts. We will not waver; we will not tire; we will not falter; and we will not fail. Peace and freedom will prevail.

Thank you. May God continue to bless America.

File photo of a Predator Unmanned Aerial Vehicle (UAV) flying above the USS Carl Vinson on a simulated navy reconnaissance flight on December 5. The Predator has a wingspan of 48.4 feet and a length of 26.7 feet, weighs approximately 1,500 pounds, costs around $3.2 million, and flies at an average speed of 70 knots. Retaliatory strikes against Afghanistan began October 7 in the first stage of the campaign against the Taliban regime.

B-52H dropping a load of M117 750-lb. bombs. The B-52H could have been part of the attack on Afghanistan at the start of the war on terrorism. Downing Street confirmed that British forces would be involved in the attacks.

British Ministry of Defense pictures of a Tomahawk land attack missile (TLAM) hitting a simulated target. The British Royal Navy submarines HMS Trafalgar and HMS Triumph fired missiles at targets in Afghanistan. It is understood that some 50 cruise missiles were launched by U.S. and U.K. forces.

Afghan opposition fighters carry grenade cup dischargers at the Bagram airport, some 19 miles from Kabul, on October 8.

Afghan opposition fighters load a mortar with shells at the Bagram airport.

U.S. F-18 fighters take off from the main deck of the USS Enterprise on October 8 as a second wave of air attacks on Afghanistan was launched with residents of Kabul reporting bombs hitting targets on the outskirts of the city.

This photo released by the Department of Defense (DOD) on October 8 shows ground crew members at an undisclosed location wave at a B-52H Stratofortress bomber as it taxis for takeoff on a strike mission against al Qaeda terrorist training camps and military installations of the Taliban regime in Afghanistan on October 7.

A U.S. F-14 fighter takes off from the main deck of the USS Enterprise early on October 9.

A Tomahawk land attack missile (TLAM) is launched from aboard the guided missile destroyer USS John Paul Jones (DDG 53) on October 8 in a strike against al Qaeda terrorist training camps and military installations of the Taliban regime in Afghanistan. The actions are part of Operation Enduring Freedom and are designed to disrupt the use of Afghanistan as a base for terrorist operations and to attack the military capability of the Taliban regime.

An Afghan opposition fighter takes position at a destroyed building at the Bagram airport, some 19 miles from Kabul, on October 9. U.S. warplanes flew combat missions over Afghanistan on the third day of an air campaign that struck the residential compound of Taliban's supreme leader and also claimed the first confirmed civilian casualties.

This image released on October 9 by the Department of Defense shows pre- and poststrike photos of the Garmabak Ghar terrorist training camp in Afghanistan. Defense Secretary Donald Rumsfeld in a briefing to the media on October 9 said that the first three days of air strikes have been successful to the point where the coalition could carry out strikes as they wished.

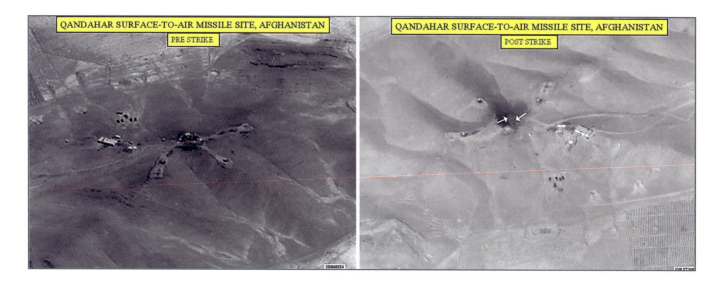

Pre- and poststrike photos of the Garmabak Ghar terrorist training camp in Afghanistan.

This TV grab from the Qatar-based satellite TV station al-Jazeera shows an explosion during an overnight air raid for the second consecutive night by U.S.-British forces on Afghanistan in retaliation for the September 11 attacks.

A B-1B Lancer drops cluster bombs during a live fire exercise on November 5. CNN quoted U.S. officials as saying retaliatory operations against Afghanistan had begun on October 7 after several loud explosions were heard in Kabul and electricity supplies were cut.

A resident riding a donkey is facing two Northern Alliance soldiers in the village of Khwaja Bahaulldin, Northern Afghanistan, some 19 miles from the Tajik border on October 10.

Northern Alliance soldiers climb up to their position, 765 yards from the Taliban lines, not far from the village of Quruq, Northern Afghanistan, about nine miles from the Tajik border.

A man sells his bread under a tent in the market in the northeastern Afghan city of Khwaja Bahaulldin under control of the anti-Taliban Northern Alliance. Afghan opposition forces said that another 40 Taliban "commanders" and some 800 soldiers had surrendered in the northeast and fighting was underway in the Samangan province.

An Afghan opposition fighter shells Taliban positions at the province of Kapiso, some 28 miles from Kabul on October 11. U.S.-led forces on Thursday launched their first afternoon raid on Kabul, extending a bombing blitz on Afghanistan.

An explosion during overnight strikes on Taliban's positions at the mountain of Bagram, near Kabul on October 11. U.S.-led forces launched their first afternoon raid on Kabul, extending a bombing blitz on Afghanistan.

PRESIDENT BUSH PAYS TRIBUTE AT PENTAGON MEMORIAL

THE PRESIDENT: Please be seated. President and Senator Clinton, thank you all for being here. We have come here to pay our respects to 125 men and women who died in the service of America. We also remember 64 passengers on a hijacked plane; those men and women, boys and girls who fell into the hands of evildoers, and also died here exactly one month ago. On September 11th, great sorrow came to our country. And from that sorrow has come great resolve. Today we are a nation awakened to the evil of terrorism and determined to destroy it. That work began the moment we were attacked; and it will continue until justice is delivered.

Americans are returning, as we must, to the normal pursuits of life. But we know that if you lost a son or daughter here, or a husband, or a wife, or a mom or dad, life will never again be as it was. The loss was sudden, and hard, and permanent. So difficult to explain. So difficult to accept. Three schoolchildren traveling with their teacher. An Army general. A budget analyst who reported to work here for 30 years. A lieutenant commander in the naval reserve who left behind a wife, a four-year-old son, and another child on the way.

One life touches so many others. One death can leave sorrow that seems almost unbearable. But to all of you who lost someone here, I want to say: You are not alone. The American people will never forget the cruelty that was done here and in New York, and in the sky over Pennsylvania.

We will never forget all the innocent people killed by the hatred of a few. We know the loneliness you feel in your loss. The entire nation shares in your sadness. And we pray for you and your loved ones. And we will always honor their memory.

The hijackers were instruments of evil who died in vain. Behind them is a cult of evil which seeks to harm the innocent and thrives on human suffering. Theirs is the worst kind of cruelty, the cruelty that is fed, not weakened, by tears. Theirs is the worst kind of violence, pure malice, while daring to claim the authority of God. We cannot fully understand the designs and power of evil. It is enough to know that evil, like goodness, exists. And in the terrorists, evil has found a willing servant. In New York, the terrorists chose as their target a symbol of America's freedom and confidence. Here, they struck a symbol of our strength in the world. And the attack on the Pentagon, on that day, was more symbolic than they knew. It was on another September 11th—September 11th, 1941—that construction on this building first began. America was just then awakening to another menace: the Nazi terror in Europe.

And on that very night, President Franklin Roosevelt spoke to the nation. The danger, he warned, has long ceased to be a mere possibility. The danger is here now. Not only from a military enemy, but from an enemy of all law, all liberty, all morality, all religion.

For us too, in the year 2001, an enemy has emerged that rejects every limit of law, morality, and religion. The terrorists have no true home in any country, or culture, or faith. They dwell in dark corners of earth. And there, we will find them.

This week, I have called the Armed

These satellite images released on October 11 by the Department of Defense shows a radio station in Afghanistan prior to air attacks (left) and after (right). The air strikes have been hitting targets in Afghanistan heavily for several days.

These satellite images released on October 11 by the Department of Defense show the Mazar-e Sharif Divisional Regiment Headquarters in Afghanistan prior to air attacks (left) and after (right).

Forces into action. One by one, we are eliminating power centers of a regime that harbors al Qaeda terrorists. We gave that regime a choice: Turn over the terrorists, or face your ruin. They chose unwisely.

The Taliban regime has brought nothing but fear and misery to the people of Afghanistan. These rulers call themselves holy men, even with their record of drawing money from heroin trafficking. They consider themselves pious and devout, while subjecting women to fierce brutality.

The Taliban has allied itself with murderers and gave them shelter. But today, for al Qaeda and the Taliban, there is no shelter. As Americans did 60 years ago, we have entered a struggle of uncertain duration. But now, as then, we can be certain of the outcome, because we have a number of decisive assets.

We have a unified country. We have the patience to fight and win on many fronts: Blocking terrorist plans, seizing their funds, arresting their networks, disrupting their communications, opposing their sponsors. And we have one more great asset in this cause: The brave men and women of the United States military.

From my first days in this office, I have felt and seen the strong spirit of the Armed Forces. I saw it at Fort Stewart, Georgia, when I first reviewed our troops as Commander-in-Chief, and looked into the faces of proud and determined soldiers. I saw it in Annapolis on a graduation day, at Camp Pendleton in California, Camp Bondsteel in Kosovo. And I have seen this spirit at the Pentagon, before and after the attack on this building.

You've responded to a great emergency with calm and courage. And for that, your country honors you. A Commander-in-Chief must know, must know that he can count on the skill and readiness of servicemen and women at every point in the chain of command. You have given me that confidence.

And I give you these commitments. The wound to this building will not be forgotten, but it will be repaired. Brick by brick, we will quickly rebuild the Pentagon. In the missions ahead for the military, you will have everything you need, every resource, every weapon, every means to assure full victory for the United States and the cause of freedom.

And I pledge to you that America will never relent on this war against terror. There will be times of swift, dramatic action. There will be times of steady, quiet progress. Over time, with patience, and precision, the terrorists will be pursued. They will be isolated, surrounded, cornered, until there is no place to run, or hide, or rest.

As military and civilian personnel in the Pentagon, you are an important part of the struggle we have entered. You know the risks of your calling, and you have willingly accepted them. You believe in our country, and our country believes in you.

Within sight of this building is Arlington Cemetery, the final resting place of many thousands who died for our country over the generations. Enemies of America have now added to these graves, and they wish to add more. Unlike our enemies, we value every life, and we mourn every loss. Yet we're not afraid. Our cause is just, and worthy of sacrifice. Our nation is strong of heart, firm of purpose. Inspired by all the courage that has come before, we will meet our moment and we will prevail.

May God bless you all, and may God bless America.

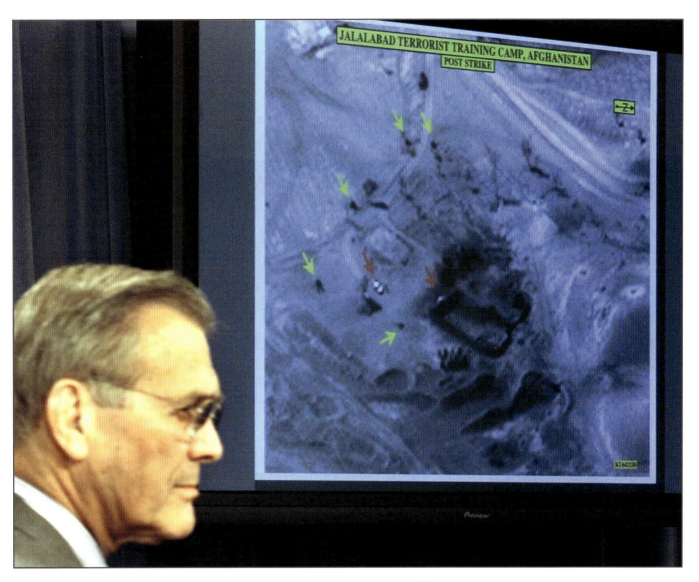

JALALABAD TERRORIST TRAINING CAMP, AFGHANISTAN
POST STRIKE

At the Pentagon on October 12, Secretary of Defense Donald Rumsfeld shows reporters footage from a U.S. aircraft that bombed Afghanistan. Rumsfeld said that the armed opposition in Afghanistan should move against the Taliban in areas where the U.S. has bombed.

A BM-21 missile launcher of Afghan opposition fighters shells Taliban positions in the province of Kapiso, some 28 miles from Kabul, on October 12. Forces pounded the Afghan capital of Kabul after a fifth night of U.S. air strikes across the country.

175

In this photo released on October 13 by the U.S. Navy, the aircraft carrier USS Carl Vinson (right) and the fast combat support ship USS Sacramento (left) steam side-by-side during a routine replenishment at sea (RAS). The Vinson is conducting flight operations against terrorist training camps and Taliban military installations in Afghanistan.

Northern Alliance soldiers shell the Taliban's positions, a few miles from the village of Dasht-i-Qala in northern Afghanistan on October 13. An opposition commander criticized Washington for not bombing the Taliban frontlines in the air and missile assault on Afghanistan now in its seventh day.

This image obtained from the Air Force on October 23 shows a B-2 Spirit Stealth Bomber, "Spirit of Alaska," from the 393rd Bomb Squadron out of Whiteman Air Force Base, MO, as it taxis out to take off. B-2s have been flying missions supporting Operation Enduring Freedom since strikes in Afghanistan began. These long-distance missions take up to 40 hours to complete.

JOINT PRESS AVAILABILITY WITH BRITISH SECRETARY OF STATE OF FOREIGN AND COMMONWEALTH AFFAIRS JACK STRAW

SECRETARY POWELL: Good morning, ladies and gentlemen. It is a great pleasure to welcome again my colleague, Foreign Minister Jack Straw, and look forward to a profitable discussion. This is a little bit different, in that we are giving the press conference before the meeting, due to schedule difficulties, and I have to get up on the Hill very quickly.

But it is a pleasure to welcome him, especially today, after we have seen such progress yesterday in the Northern Ireland peace process, and I want to extend my congratulations to Jack and to Prime Minister Tony Blair and to the Irish Prime Minister Bertie Ahern, for this step forward, and it shows what can happen when one remains persistent and with a determination to solve what appear to be intractable problems.

I am sure that the Minister and I will also have occasion to talk a great deal about the situation in Afghanistan. And let me take this opportunity to again thank the British Government for the strong support that they have given to us in this time of crisis since the 11th of September. As always, we can count on the United Kingdom, and they have come through again. And likewise, we deeply appreciate their military contribution to the campaign.

But more than just these political-military things, we deeply appreciate the outpouring of support that we received from the British people during this time of challenge and crisis. We also had a chance to extend our condolences to Her Majesty's citizens who were lost in the World Trade Center as well.

We will be speaking, I am sure, also about the future of Afghanistan. The Foreign Minister gave a very important speech earlier this week that talked about what we have to do with respect to putting in place a broad-based government and what we have to do with respect to helping the people of Afghanistan get on a path to a better life in a post-Taliban regime. And I am sure there are a full range of European issues, NATO issues, that we will also have a chance to discuss in the next hour or so. So, Jack, welcome. It is always a pleasure to have you, sir.

FOREIGN MINISTER STRAW: Colin, thank you very much indeed for that welcome. I am delighted to be here. The last time I was in this room was towards the end of June, in rather more benign circumstances. Since then, we have had the atrocities on the 11th of September. And I think it is worth my underlining to you and to the American people the huge admiration we have in the United Kingdom for the steadfastness and courage which was shown on the 11th of September by so many people in New York and Washington and elsewhere, for the steadfastness and patience and wisdom shown by your President, by you, sir, and by members of your administration for all the work that is now being done by United States forces as well, and for the fact that whilst it's—and I can say this as somebody who has only ever been a politician—politicians, sometimes put their reputations but no more on the line. It is members of our armed forces who put their lives on the line, and we expect great things from them and we get great things from them.

You have been very kind, as your President has, about the sentiment and the feeling in the United Kingdom. It was instinctive. It was just there, because we feel part of almost of a family. But it was also instinctive because of a recognition that, on two occasions, in a very short space of time, the United States came to our aid. We would not enjoy the freedoms which we do in the United Kingdom and elsewhere in Europe and throughout the rest of the world without the selfless aid of the United States at our time of need. So it is the least, the very least, that we can do.

Secretary Powell has gone through the agenda that we will be discussing during our lunch. Obviously, [it] includes the future of Afghanistan. You were good enough to mention the speech which I made two days ago. We have done a great deal of thinking on both sides of the Atlantic about the future of Afghanistan. You can't say exactly what form of government it should have, but I think we can see the building blocks that are necessary to secure a stable and safe future for that country.

On the issue of terrorism, thank you, too, for what you have said about the Northern Ireland peace process. That, I think, is a very good example about how, from very, very dark circumstances—and we have had to live with terrorism—the people of Northern Ireland, much worse, have had to live with terrorism for year after year after year, killed hundreds of people. But from very, very dark beginnings, it is possible to see a light and then, provided the process is kept going and kept going through those difficulties, you can achieve a result. And that, I believe, is what has happened. Thank you.

U.S. GROUND FORCES HELPING NORTHERN ALLIANCE

A "modest" number of U.S. troops are on the ground supporting the Northern Alliance in Afghanistan, Defense Secretary Donald H. Rumsfeld said October 30.

In a joint press conference with British Defense Minister Geoffrey Hoon, Rumsfeld said the Americans are on the ground only in the north of the country. "We've had others on the ground who have come in and out, in the south," he said.

Rumsfeld said the U.S. personnel are uniformed service members who are assisting with resupply and communications liaison with some portions of the Northern Alliance. They are also "assisting with targeting and providing the kind of specific information that is helping with the air effort," he said. The presence of these personnel has improved the effectiveness of the air campaign against frontline Taliban and al Qaeda forces, he added.

Department of Defense officials said the U.S. forces have been on the ground for only a few days.

"It has taken time to get the kinds of help on the ground that can provide the specificity needed to provide good targeting from the air," Rumsfeld said.

The effectiveness of the air-ground coordination has been uneven because U.S. forces are not currently with each of the various opposition elements in the country, he said. "It will be more effective in areas where we do have people working with those forces," Rumsfeld said.

He said the ground commitment may grow. "It is true we have nothing like the ground forces we had in World War II or Korea or the Gulf War," he said. "Nor have we ruled that out."

Rumsfeld met with Hoon to discuss U.S.-British strategies against terrorism. The British have been in the action against al Qaeda and the Taliban from the start. The British have allowed U.S. forces to use the Indian Ocean base of Diego Garcia. British forces fired Tomahawk cruise missiles at terrorist training camps at the start of the air war. In addition, British aerial refueling tankers and reconnaissance aircraft are supporting U.S. strike aircraft. "Last Friday we announced that all of Britain's aircraft carriers reequipped to carry helicopters, will join these forces along with an assault ship, two escorts, Royal Marines, naval auxiliary vessels, and maritime reconnaissance and transport aircraft," Hoon said. This means about 4,200 British service members are committed to Operation Veritas, the United Kingdom's military contribution to Operation Enduring Freedom.

An F/A-18 "Hornet" from the "Mighty Shrikes" of Strike Fighter Squadron Nine Four (VFA-94) fires flares during a training mission on October 31 in the skies over Afghanistan. Flares are part of the aircraft's defense against surface-to-air and air-to-air infrared (IR) heat-seeking missile attacks. IR missiles follow a heat source. The heat created by the flare should burn hotter than the aircraft engine and attract the incoming missile away from the aircraft. VFA-94 is assigned to Carrier Air wing Eleven aboard USS Carl Vinson.

The HMAS Sydney leaves its mooring in Darwin on October 31 to start a six-month tour of duty with the U.S.-led coalition in the Indian Ocean. Australia has committed 1,550 Defense force personnel to the campaign against terrorism.

President George W. Bush speaks to the media on November 7 with British Prime Minister Tony Blair by his side. Blair is also having dinner with Bush at the White House later that day to discuss the current U.S. and British military operations in Afghanistan.

This photo released by the Department of Defense on November 16 shows U.S. special forces troops riding horseback as they work with members of the Northern Alliance in Afghanistan during Operation Enduring Freedom.

Italian soldiers of the San Marco battalion line up on the aircraft carrier Garibaldi at the port of Taranto on November 18 as four Italian Navy ships are about to set sail to join Operation Enduring Freedom. The aircraft carrier Garibaldi, the frigates Zeffiro and Aviere, and the supply ship Etna, with 1,400 crew and military personnel, will join the campaign against terrorism.

RUMSFELD THANKS SPECIAL OPERATORS DURING BRAGG VISIT

Defense Secretary Donald Rumsfeld was a hit among service members and their families, here. The secretary wisecracked his way into their hearts—mostly at the expense of the media contingent present—during a pre-Thanksgiving visit. Rumsfeld visited troops here and received operations and capabilities briefings and demonstrations. Troops who briefed the secretary had apparently been instructed to begin by thoroughly identifying themselves. Each soldier who spoke to Rumsfeld gave his name, job, age, and hometown.

The secretary returned the favor when he finally took to the podium in the afternoon to speak to an assembled crowd. "I think I'd better do the same thing," he told the group. "I'm Don Rumsfeld; I'm 69 years old; I've been married 47 years, if you can believe that." To which he received a thunderous applause.

He called the Fort Bragg troops "some of the most outstanding young men and women in the armed forces of the United States of America."

Rumsfeld told the troops their welfare is always on his mind. "I don't suppose there's a day goes by that I don't keep track of what you folks are doing in the North of Afghanistan (and) are doing in the south of Afghanistan," he said, "It gives me immense pride to be able to say to each of you how much respect I have for you and what you do."

Several hundred special operations service members are with opposition groups in Afghanistan. Still others are working to track down Osama bin Laden's al Qaeda supporters and their Taliban supporters. Rumsfeld said that while the air strikes against the terror targets in Afghanistan were effective, they are "very difficult to do unless you've got troops on the ground."

He told the troops they have "well earned" their outstanding reputation. "The world knows why when the president dials 911, it rings right here in Fayetteville," Rumsfeld said.

He had a special Thanksgiving thank you for the service members. "Tomorrow, families across America will sit down to Thanksgiving dinner (and will) give thanks for the blessings and benefits of freedom," Rumsfeld told them. "As sure as we are standing here today you can be certain that as they reflect they will be thanking God for all you do. You willingly put your lives at risk to defend our country and our freedom in far off places all across the globe."

He then opened the floor to questions "from anybody, except maybe the press," he said. But the troops lived up to their "silent killers" reputation and when none of the soldiers had a question, Rumsfeld joked about that, too. "How long have you been sitting here?" he quipped. "That is amazing. This is the most unusual group I've ever met. I guess I will take questions from the press."

When a reporter asked for an update on actions in Afghanistan, Rumsfeld said: "If you're asking if I can talk about what's going on on the ground, the answer is 'I could,'" and left it at that. And when Rumsfeld was ready to take the last question, he told the chagrined television reporter he was going to let the crowd judge how good of a question it was. The crowd roared.

The secretary took every opportunity to tell the troops how much they're appreciated. "It is absolutely thrilling to be here to see these folks and to be able to look them in the eye and say thank you," he said.

Earlier in the day, Rumsfeld watched demonstrations and displays by special operations forces. The 3rd Special Forces Group, Army Rangers, Air Force combat controllers, and Navy SEALS, among others, displayed their equipment, answered questions, and displayed their prowess.

Two Marine CH-46 helicopters bank as they prepare to land aboard the USS Peleliu, an Amphibious Assault Ship (LH5) sailing the northern Arabian Sea. The helicopters are ferrying Marine and Navy personnel to the ship in order to lead the landing assault and establish a significant U.S. military presence on the ground in southern Afghanistan. Marines took command of a secret airstrip in southern Afghanistan on November 25.

A U.S. Marine rides atop a humvee mounted with a TOW antitank missile during a patrol near Camp Rhino in southern Afghanistan during a period of heightened alert on December 7. The Hunter-Killer teams are members of the 15th Marine Expeditionary Unit operating in southern Afghanistan.

TALIBAN SURRENDERING KANDAHAR, U.S. FORCES IN FIREFIGHTS

Taliban forces are surrendering in their stronghold of Kandahar, said Army Gen. Tommy Franks, but U.S. forces continue to engage armed enemy fighters attempting to leave the area.

Franks, commander of U.S. Central Command, briefed reporters today at the Pentagon and his headquarters at MacDill Air Force Base, FL, through an unusual teleconference.

He said U.S. Marines have been interdicting roads via airpower and direct fire. Special operations forces are with opposition forces also closing off the city. Franks said the Americans have engaged in several firefights but that he has not seen large numbers of armed Taliban leaving Kandahar.

He said the noose is tightening around Taliban and al Qaeda leaders in Afghanistan. He said he has no reason to believe Taliban leader Mullah Mohammed Omar has escaped Kandahar nor that Afghanistan's interim Prime Minister Hamid Karzai had engineered a deal to let Omar escape.

Franks likened the situation around Kandahar to that around Mazar-e Sharif in November. Reports from the city are sketchy and Taliban forces are attempting to blend into the countryside. He said it will take two or three days before some control is established in the city.

He said it is possible more U.S. troops will be needed in the country soon. He also said he will make decisions in the next few days on moving around troops already deployed in Afghanistan. "Everything is on the table," he said.

Franks said fighting still rages in the Tora Bora cave complex south of Jalalabad. He said U.S. and opposition forces are doing their best in the "very rugged terrain" to ensure Osama bin Laden and other al Qaeda leaders do not escape across the border into Pakistan. DoD officials said they believe bin Laden is still in the country.

"His options are limited," said an official. "Who is going to harbor him and invite U.S. response?"

Franks said he expects the Friendship Bridge between Uzbekistan and Afghanistan will open in the next two or three days. Opening the bridge would speed aid relief to the northern part of Afghanistan. Franks said Uzbekistani officials are concerned about the security environment in Afghanistan and about the safety of the bridge.

Franks spoke at the podium accompanied by British Air Marshal G. E. Stirrup and Australian Brigadier Kenneth James Gillespie. The United Kingdom and Australia have fought since the beginning of the campaign with the coalition against terrorism. Franks said the two men represent more than 50 nations engaged in the effort. At MacDill, 230 representatives from more than 20 nations are "a very visible sign of the international commitment to our overall effort," he said.

The fighting in Afghanistan is entering a critical phase, Franks said, adding that any idea the U.S. effort is diminishing is wrong. He said his command is watching other nations in its area of operations that the State Department says encourage and harbor terrorists. He said he's encouraged by circumstances to date.

"We're progressing, progressing well, but we have a long way to go," Franks said. "We're tightening the noose, but the way ahead has been correctly described as one where we'll find a dirty environment and a very dangerous environment."

U.S. Special Operation Capable (SOC) Marines with the 26th Marines Expeditionary Unit (MEU), load their equipment on a truck as they arrive at an undisclosed location in a country that the military requested "not be named" late on December 11. Three U.S. amphibious ships, part of the 15th and the 26th MEU, are sailing off the Pakistani coasts.

U.S. Marines form up at a staging area near Kandahar as they await to depart with light armored vehicles and humvees en route to Kandahar to take control of the airfield on December 13. Some 200 U.S. Marines backed by dozens of armored vehicles moved in before dawn on December 14 to occupy the airport and started sweeping it for mines and booby traps.

RUMSFELD VISITS AFGHANISTAN, MEETS WITH U.S. TROOPS

Defense Secretary Donald H. Rumsfeld met with U.S. troops and Afghan leaders during a visit to this former Soviet base, December 16.

Rumsfeld met with soldiers of the 10th Mountain Division, other soldiers providing logistics and Air Force personnel who are manning the "bare bones" base. He also met with Hamid Karsai, the Afghan leader who will be the interim prime minister of the country, and Fahim Kahn, who will be the defense minister in the new government. The meetings were held in a bombed-out hanger on the base. Rumsfeld said his talks with the Afghan leaders went well and that Karsai was very appreciative of the United States. Rumsfeld related that Karsai said the United States gave Afghan opposition forces "the opportunity that we wanted to liberate ourselves for a second time." The first time was the mujahedin victory over the Soviet Union in 1989.

Rumsfeld told Karsai the United States would continue to support the opposition forces and that the United States had no territorial designs on Afghanistan. "The United States has done very well so far," said Imran, a Karsai aid. "The [American servicemen] who serve with our forces know our culture and respect it. The fighters here are few and also respect the people."

He contrasted the small U.S. footprint in Afghanistan to the Soviet occupation. "They were everywhere," he said of the Soviets. "You [are] doing this right," he told the American contingent.

All of the men who accompanied Karsai or Khan carried weapons of some sort, including one man who waited outside the meeting carrying a rocket-propelled grenade.

Rumsfeld said the meetings with the Afghan leaders were important. He said they allowed Karsai to understand what President Bush and Rumsfeld are thinking, and gave Rumsfeld a chance to size up Karsai.

Rumsfeld toured the base and then held a "town hall meeting" with U.S. service members. He said the military services would undoubtedly establish some sort of rotation policy for duty in Afghanistan.

The United States will not leave until the mission is accomplished, he said. The secretary told service members the mission will be finished in Afghanistan when the Taliban leadership is killed or captured, the al Qaeda leaders and all their fighters are killed or captured, and the country is no longer a training ground for terror groups.

Rumsfeld answered a couple of questions on the proposed security force for Kabul. He said the force will not be a United Nations peacekeeping force, but will work under a UN mandate. The United Kingdom would lead the force with help from Turkey and Germany, Rumsfeld said. "It will be no more than 3,000 to 5,000 [service members]," he said. "It is only to be based in Kabul, but there is talk of expanding it to other cities."

The United States will not participate in the main body of the peacekeeping force. Rumsfeld said the United States would provide intelligence and airlift for the effort and will provide a quick reaction force that can be used if needed.

Rumsfeld told the troops he was grateful for their service. "Every day I've watched what's going on in this country and what you folks are doing with great pride at the skill, the training, the discipline, and the dedication that you all bring to what you are doing," he said.

United States Marines, shown through a night vision scope, escort battle field detainees into a detention center at the Kandahar International Airport on December 18.

MYERS: SUCCESS SO FAR, BUT TERROR WAR FAR FROM OVER

Good planning, patience, and the willpower to win have enabled U.S. and coalition forces to defeat or neutralize al Qaeda terrorist forces and their Taliban supporters throughout most of Afghanistan, DoD's senior military officer said today.

Some of the military success achieved thus far in Afghanistan "is attributable to the strategy, which was designed basically by Central Command, [with] a lot of help from the intelligence agencies," Air Force Gen. Richard B. Myers, the chairman of the Joint Chiefs of Staff, told reporters at NATO headquarters here.

Besides planning, "patience and the cooperation from our allies and the ability to use the full spectrum of U.S. military capabilities" assisted in achieving success thus far against the terrorists in Afghanistan, Myers remarked.

"Certainly, jointness was [also] a big part" of the military success in Afghanistan, he added.

However, the antiterrorist campaign in Afghanistan isn't over, the general noted. He added that the war against worldwide terrorism "is going to take a long time,"

requiring "continuous effort" by the United States and its allies.

"This is a global war on terrorism," Myers said, quoting Defense Secretary Donald H. Rumsfeld. The United States and its allies, Myers added, will continue to carry the fight to "terrorists and their networks, [and] those that support them."

Also targeted are "those that conduct research [for] or produce weapons of mass destruction" that could fall into the hands of terrorists, Myers noted.

Myers noted that military action isn't the only option that can be employed in the war on global terrorism. Financial, diplomatic, law enforcement, or intelligence options are also available to America and its allies, he added.

"Obviously, in Afghanistan we're focused on the military action; that's what is the most visible," Myers said, adding that he wouldn't speculate where, besides Afghanistan, the war on terrorism might continue.

U.S. and coalition forces in Afghanistan continue the search for al Qaeda leader Osama bin Laden, Myers said. He remarked that he didn't know if bin Laden is still in the mountainous Tora Bora region, if he has been injured or killed, or if he has left Afghanistan.

"We will continue to follow all leads, though," Myers emphasized, adding, "It is not just bin Laden we're after."

Bin Laden "has handfuls of lieutenants we want to go after," the general noted.

"We know who they are, they already have rewards on their heads, and we'll follow them wherever they go," he concluded.

Rumsfeld and Myers had completed two days of NATO defense ministerial meetings today. The defense secretary and the general both arrived in Brussels on December 17. Rumsfeld arrived in Brussels near the end of a six-day trip, which had included a December 16 stop at Bagram Air Base, about 20 miles from Kabul, the capital of Afghanistan.

After the press conference, Rumsfeld flew on to Washington, while Myers continues eastward for a holiday-season visit with U.S. troops serving in parts of South Asia and the Middle East. The general is slated to return to Washington, December 24.

This image obtained on January 4, 2002, from the U.S. Navy shows a U.S. Marine with the 26th Marine Expeditionary Unit (Special Operations Capable), Battalion Landing Team 3/6, providing small-arms support while an advance team conducts a Cordon and Search Raid at a suspected al Qaeda hideout in the Helmand Province of Afghanistan on January 1.

In this photo released January 18 by the Department of Defense, al Qaeda and Taliban detainees in orange jumpsuits sit in a holding area under the surveillance of U.S. military police at Camp X-Ray at Naval Base Guantanamo Bay, Cuba, during in-processing to the temporary detention facility on January 11. The detainees, captured in Afghanistan during Operation Enduring Freedom, are given a basic physical exam by a doctor.

This U.S. Navy photo released February 1 shows U.S. Navy Seals on January 14 during a search and destroy mission in which they discovered a large cache of munitions in one of more than 50 caves explored in the Zhawar Kili area. Used by al Qaeda and Taliban forces, the caves and above-ground complexes were subsequently destroyed through air strikes called in by the Seals.

WOLFOWITZ: WORLD MUST ACT NOW TO PREVENT EVIL

The world must act now to prevent terrorist networks from unleashing even more devastating evil than they did on September 11, U.S. Deputy Defense Secretary Paul Wolfowitz said today in Germany.

"We cannot afford to wait," he stressed in remarks prepared for delivery at the Munich Conference on European Security Policy. For too long, he said, the international community has accepted terrorism as an "ugly fact of life."

"People spoke frequently of retaliation, but rarely acted," Wolfowitz said. "And when they did act, it was more often against the lower-level perpetrators of terrorist acts than against those who were ultimately responsible."

September 11 changed all of that.

What happened on that day, "terrible though it was, is but a pale shadow of what will happen if terrorists use weapons of massive destruction," he said. "No one who has seen the images of September 11 can doubt that our response must be wide-ranging, nor should anyone doubt the far greater destruction terrorists could wreak with weapons of greater power."

Documents found in the caves of Afghanistan reveal the scope of what the world faces, he noted. U.S. officials discovered diagrams of U.S. nuclear power plants and water facilities, maps of cities, and descriptions of landmarks—not just in America, but also around the world—along with detailed instructions for making chemical weapons.

The United States now considers all nations that harbor, finance, train, or equip terrorists "hostile regimes" that will be held accountable, Wolfowitz said.

"Those who plotted in the caves share a kinship with states who seek to export terror," he said. "They pose a clear and direct threat to international security that could prove far more cataclysmic than what we have experienced already."

Wolfowitz said President Bush has launched a campaign to hunt down terrorists relentlessly and to deny them the sanctuaries they need to plan and organize. The U.S. campaign is not just a military one, he said, but also integrates diplomacy, intelligence, law enforcement, and financial influence to disrupt and defeat the global terrorist network.

"Our approach has to aim at prevention and not merely punishment," he said. "We are at war."

U.S. officials want countries that stand for peace, security, and the rule of law to join in the struggle between good and evil, he said. Countries that tolerate or support terrorism will face consequences.

"As President Bush said last Tuesday, 'Make no mistake about it: If they do not act, America will,'" Wolfowitz said.

The war on terrorism will be a long struggle requiring the contributions of many nations in "flexible coalitions," he said. U.S. policy has been to accept help from countries on whatever basis is most comfortable to them. Some join publicly; others have chosen "quiet and discrete forms of cooperation."

"We recognize that it is best for each country to characterize how they are helping, instead of doing it for them," Wolfowitz said. "Ultimately, this maximizes their cooperation and our effectiveness."

In Afghanistan, he noted, America's most important coalition partners were the Afghans themselves.

"Because of the historic Afghan hostility to foreign invaders, we strived from the beginning to keep our footprint small and emphasized that we were not in Afghanistan to stay," he explained. "Instead, we leveraged the desire of the Afghan people to be liberated from the Taliban and to be rid of the foreign terrorists who brought so much destruction to their country."

Wolfowitz called on European allies to help expand the alliance against terrorism to include the Muslim world. He said the fight against terrorism is not just a fight of the Western countries, but of all who aspire to peace and freedom throughout the world.

Based on his own experience as U.S. ambassador to Indonesia in the 1980s, the country with the largest Muslim population in the world, Wolfowitz said he knows the majority of the world's Muslims "abhor terrorism" and the way terrorists "have not only hijacked airplanes but also attempted to hijack one of the world's great religions."

To win the war against terrorism, he said, "we have to reach out to the hundreds of millions of moderate and tolerant people in the Muslim world, including the Arab world. They are on the frontline of the struggle against terrorism.

"By helping them to stand up against the terrorists without fear," he said, "we help ourselves. Equally important, we help to lay the foundations for a better world after the battle against terrorism has been won."

U.S. Marines stand in front of a C-130 transport aircraft at Kandahar airport on January 23 before their departure for home. About 3,000 Marines are being replaced by Army soldiers.

This photo released February 19 shows U.S. Navy Seals examining the entrance to one of more than 50 caves explored in the Zhawar Kili area of Afghanistan January 14 during a search and destroy mission.

This January 15 photo released by the U.S. Navy on January 16 shows tunnels discovered by the U.S. Marines being destroyed in Kandahar, Afghanistan. U.S. Marines from Battalion Landing Team 3/6, 26th Marine Expeditionary Unit.

Secretary of State Colin Powell (right) chats with U.S. Marines during his visit to the U.S. embassy in Kabul on January 17. Powell's visit to Afghanistan is the first by an American state secretary since the visit by Henry Kissinger 25 years ago. At top left in the background is U.S. Ambassador to Afghanistan Ryan Crocker.

Epilogue

President Barack Obama delivers a statement in the East Room of the White House on the mission against Osama bin Laden, May 1, 2011. (Official White House Photo by Pete Souza)

PRESIDENT OBAMA ADDRESSES THE NATION MAY 1, 2011

THE PRESIDENT: Good evening. Tonight, I can report to the American people and to the world that the United States has conducted an operation that killed Osama bin Laden, the leader of al Qaeda, and a terrorist who's responsible for the murder of thousands of innocent men, women, and children.

It was nearly 10 years ago that a bright September day was darkened by the worst attack on the American people in our history. The images of 9/11 are seared into our national memory -- hijacked planes cutting through a cloudless September sky; the Twin Towers collapsing to the ground; black smoke billowing up from the Pentagon; the wreckage of Flight 93 in Shanksville, Pennsylvania, where the actions of heroic citizens saved even more heartbreak and destruction.

And yet we know that the worst images are those that were unseen to the world. The empty seat at the dinner table. Children who were forced to grow up without their mother or their father. Parents who would never know the feeling of their child's embrace. Nearly 3,000 citizens taken from us, leaving a gaping hole in our hearts.

On September 11, 2001, in our time of grief, the American people came together. We offered our neighbors a hand, and we offered the wounded our blood. We reaffirmed our ties to each other, and our love of community and country. On that day, no matter where we came from, what God we prayed to, or what race or ethnicity we were, we were united as one American family.

We were also united in our resolve to protect our nation and to bring those who committed this vicious attack to justice. We quickly learned that the 9/11 attacks were carried out by al Qaeda -- an organization headed by Osama bin Laden, which had openly declared war on the United States and was committed to killing innocents in our country and around the globe. And so we went to war against al Qaeda to protect our citizens, our friends, and our allies.

Over the last 10 years, thanks to the tireless and heroic work of our military and our counterterrorism professionals, we've made great strides in that effort. We've disrupted terrorist attacks and strengthened our homeland defense. In Afghanistan, we removed the Taliban government, which had given bin Laden and al Qaeda safe haven and support. And around the globe, we worked with our friends and allies to capture or kill scores of al Qaeda terrorists, including several who were a part of the 9/11 plot.

Yet Osama bin Laden avoided capture and escaped across the Afghan border into Pakistan. Meanwhile, al Qaeda continued to operate from along that border and operate through its affiliates across the world.

And so shortly after taking office, I directed Leon Panetta, the director of the CIA, to make the killing or capture of bin Laden the top priority of our war against al Qaeda, even as we continued our broader efforts to disrupt, dismantle, and defeat his network.

Then, last August, after years of painstaking work by our intelligence community, I was briefed on a possible lead to bin Laden. It was far from certain, and it took many months to run this thread to ground. I met repeatedly with my national security

President Barack Obama edits his remarks in the Oval Office prior to making a televised statement detailing the mission against Osama bin Laden, May 1, 2011.

team as we developed more information about the possibility that we had located bin Laden hiding within a compound deep inside of Pakistan. And finally, last week, I determined that we had enough intelligence to take action, and authorized an operation to get Osama bin Laden and bring him to justice.

Today, at my direction, the United States launched a targeted operation against that compound in Abbottabad, Pakistan. A small team of Americans carried out the operation with extraordinary courage and capability. No Americans were harmed. They took care to avoid civilian casualties. After a firefight, they killed Osama bin Laden and took custody of his body.

For over two decades, bin Laden has been al Qaeda's leader and symbol, and has continued to plot attacks against our country and our friends and allies. The death of bin Laden marks the most significant achievement to date in our nation's effort to defeat al Qaeda.

Yet his death does not mark the end of our effort. There's no doubt that al Qaeda will continue to pursue attacks against us. We must -- and we will -- remain vigilant at home and abroad.

As we do, we must also reaffirm that the United States is not -- and never will be -- at war with Islam. I've made clear, just as President Bush did shortly after 9/11, that our war is not against Islam. Bin Laden was not a Muslim leader; he was a mass murderer of Muslims. Indeed, al Qaeda has slaughtered scores of Muslims in many countries, including our own. So his demise should be welcomed by all who believe in peace and human dignity.

Over the years, I've repeatedly made clear that we would take action within Pakistan if we knew where bin Laden was. That is what we've done. But it's important to note that our counterterrorism cooperation with Pakistan helped lead us to bin Laden and the compound where he was hiding. Indeed, bin Laden had declared war against Pakistan as well, and ordered attacks against the Pakistani people.

Tonight, I called President Zardari, and my team has also spoken with their Pakistani counterparts. They agree that this is a good and historic day for both of our nations. And going forward, it is essential that Pakistan continue to join us in the fight against al Qaeda and its affiliates.

The American people did not choose this fight. It came to our shores, and started with the senseless slaughter of our citizens. After nearly 10 years of service, struggle, and sacrifice, we know well the costs of war. These efforts weigh on me every time I, as Commander-in-Chief, have to sign a letter to a family that has lost a loved one, or look into the eyes of a service member who's been gravely wounded.

So Americans understand the costs of war.

Yet as a country, we will never tolerate our security being threatened, nor stand idly by when our people have been killed. We will be relentless in defense of our citizens and our friends and allies. We will be true to the values that make us who we are. And on nights like this one, we can say to those families who have lost loved ones to al Qaeda's terror: Justice has been done.

Tonight, we give thanks to the countless intelligence and counterterrorism professionals who've worked tirelessly to achieve this outcome. The American people do not see their work, nor know their names. But tonight, they feel the satisfaction of their work and the result of their pursuit of justice.

We give thanks for the men who carried out this operation, for they exemplify the professionalism, patriotism, and unparalleled courage of those who serve our country. And they are part of a generation that has borne the heaviest share of the burden since that September day.

Finally, let me say to the families who lost loved ones on 9/11 that we have never forgotten your loss, nor wavered in our commitment to see that we do whatever it takes to prevent another attack on our shores.

And tonight, let us think back to the sense of unity that prevailed on 9/11. I know that it has, at times, frayed. Yet today's achievement is a testament to the greatness of our country and the determination of the American people.

The cause of securing our country is not complete. But tonight, we are once again reminded that America can do whatever we set our mind to. That is the story of our history, whether it's the pursuit of prosperity for our people, or the struggle for equality for all our citizens; our commitment to stand up for our values abroad, and our sacrifices to make the world a safer place.

Let us remember that we can do these things not just because of wealth or power, but because of who we are: one nation, under God, indivisible, with liberty and justice for all.

Thank you. May God bless you. And may God bless the United States of America.

END   11:44 P.M. EDT

President Barack Obama and Vice President Joe Biden, along with members of the national security team, receive an update on the mission against Osama bin Laden in the Situation Room of the White House, May 1, 2011. Seated, from left, are: Brigadier General Marshall B. "Brad" Webb, Assistant Commanding General, Joint Special Operations Command; Deputy National Security Advisor Denis McDonough; Secretary of State Hillary Rodham Clinton; and Secretary of Defense Robert Gates. Standing, from left, are: Admiral Mike Mullen, Chairman of the Joint Chiefs of Staff; National Security Advisor Tom Donilon; Chief of Staff Bill Daley; Tony Binken, National Security Advisor to the Vice President; Audrey Tomason Director for Counterterrorism; John Brennan, Assistant to the President for Homeland Security and Counterterrorism; and Director of National Intelligence James Clapper. Please note: a classified document seen in this photograph has been obscured.

WASHINGTON (NNS) -- Osama bin Laden received a Muslim ceremony as he was buried at sea, a senior defense official said in Washington, D.C., May 2.

The religious rites were performed aboard the aircraft carrier USS Carl Vinson (CVN 70) in the North Arabian Sea and occurred within 24 hours of the terrorist leader's death, said the official. "Preparations for at-sea [burial] began at 1:10 a.m. Eastern Standard Time and were completed at 2 a.m.," said the official. The burial followed traditional Muslim burial customs, and bin Laden's body was washed and placed in a white sheet, said the official. "The body was placed in a weighted bag. A military officer read prepared religious remarks, which were translated into Arabic by a native speaker," the official added. Afterward, bin Laden's body was placed onto a flat board, which was then elevated upward on one side and the body slid off into the sea. The deceased terrorist was buried at sea because no country would accept bin Laden's remains, a senior defense official said. Central Intelligence Agency (CIA) and Defense Department officials are sure it was the body of bin Laden. CIA specialists compared photos of the body with known photos of bin Laden and said with 95-percent certainty it was the terrorist leader, a senior intelligence official said. In addition, bin Laden's wife identified the al-Qaida leader by name while the strike team was still in the compound, said the intelligence official. CIA and other specialists in the intelligence community "performed the initial DNA analysis matching a virtually 100-percent DNA match of the body against the DNA of several of bin Laden's family members," the official added.